THE GOOD, THE BAD, AND THE UGLY
NEW YORK GIANTS

HEART-POUNDING, JAW-DROPPING, AND GUT-WRENCHING MOMENTS FROM NEW YORK GIANTS HISTORY

Michael Benson

TRIUMPH
BOOKS

Triumph Books and colophon are registered trademarks of Random House, Inc.

Library of Congress Cataloging-in-Publication Data

Benson, Michael, 1956–.
   The good, the bad, and the ugly New York Giants / by Michael Benson.
      p. cm.
   Includes bibliographical references.
   ISBN-13: 978-1-60078-012-7 (alk. paper)
   ISBN-10: 1-60078-012-1 (alk. paper)
    1. New York Giants (Football team)—History. I. Title.

GV956.N4B46 2007
796.332'64097471—dc22

                                                    2007018204

This book is available in quantity at special discounts for your group or organization. For further information, contact:

Triumph Books
542 South Dearborn Street
Suite 750
Chicago, Illinois 60605
(312) 939-3330
Fax (312) 663-3557

Printed in U.S.A.
ISBN-13: 978-1-60078-012-7
Design by Patricia Frey
All photos courtesy of AP/Wide World Photos except where otherwise indicated.

To all the football giants,
young and old

CONTENTS

ACKNOWLEDGMENTS

Pat Hanlon, Giants director of public relations; Mario Prosperino, manager of NFL sales and services at Getty Images; Langston Rogers, public relations department at the University of Mississippi; my agent, Jake Elwell; my wife, Lisa Grasso; author David Henry Jacobs; Gary Goldstein, Norman Jacobs, and the Starlog Group of magazines; photographer George Napolitano; Philip Semrau, Nathan Versace, Keith Brenner, Anne Darrigan, Eddie and Cate Behringer, Larry Beck, Scott Frommer, Erin Mainey, Paul Johnson, and Carl Soloway.

THE GOOD

There have been more than 40 Super Bowls, and the Giants have won two of them. Maybe that doesn't seem like a tremendous stat, but considering the size of the NFL, it still means that Big Blue has won more than its share. And so we start with "The Good," stories of Giants who wear rings.

PHIL SIMMS: PRACTICALLY PERFECT IN EVERY WAY

In the long run Super Bowl XXI was the climax of the Phil Simms story. Not the end of the story, for sure, but the high point for the injury-prone quarterback, the much-maligned first-round pick out of—is that a typo?—Morehead State. When they announced his pick in the 1979 NFL draft the Giants fans in attendance booed heartily. They booed vociferously and with gusto. They booed with vociferous gusto! The fans attending the draft had had their hearts set on Jack Thompson, the "Throwin' Samoan" from Washington State University, who ended up going to the Bengals.

It was at age 31, in his eighth year with the Giants, that Phil Simms stepped onto the biggest stage of his life. Super Bowl XXI was played in a jam-packed Rose Bowl and before a record TV audience. Under those ultimate circumstances, Simms gave a near-perfect performance: he connected on 88 percent of his passes, gained 268 yards through the air, and completed three touchdown passes. It was a vindication for all of those who believed in him all along, and it was proof positive that the finger-pointers were wrong.

His completion rate was not just the best ever for a quarterback in a Super Bowl, but also for quarterbacks who threw the ball 15 or more times in a game. Simms's completion rate was the highest in NFL postseason history.

So where's the TV movie? He had transcended adversity and risen from a small school in Kentucky to the pinnacle of his profession. Even at the end, when he couldn't have been a bigger football hero, a football hero of Namathian proportions, he still shared camera time with a young Bill Parcells, who in 1985 had become the first football coach in the history of football coaches to have Gatorade poured over his head by his players in joyous celebration. By Super Bowl Sunday, Parcells's Gatorade bath had become a Giants tradition, and by the following season, the practice had caught on anywhere there was football, big games, coaches, and Gatorade.

BIRTH OF THE GATORADE SHOWER

Six weeks into the 1985 season, coach Bill Parcells was getting on Jim Burt's case, driving him, embarrassing him, getting inside his head. When the mind games worked and Burt played great the next Sunday to help the Giants win, Burt got back at his coach by dumping the Gatorade on Parcells during the final seconds of the game.

At first Burt's teammates and the spectators were stunned, thinking it insubordination, a sure sign of disrespect. But Parcells laughed and took it in good humor. The next week the Giants won again, and this time, Burt and Harry Carson dumped the Gatorade on Parcells together. By that time the dumping of the Gatorade was seen as a symbol of victory and, ironically, of the coach's leadership.

The Gatorade shower of the head coach became a Giants tradition and eventually caught on throughout the world of football.

Bill Parcells is still revered by Giants fans for bringing two Super Bowl victories to New York. He was also the first-ever recipient of a Gatorade bath—courtesy here of linebacker Harry Carson, cleverly disguised as a Rose Bowl security officer.

But we start with the end of the story. Let's go back and find out how Phil Simms got to the mountaintop—and a very *good* mountaintop it was.

Philip Martin Simms was born on November 3, 1955, in Lebanon, Kentucky. He grew up in Louisville, and when it came time to go to college, he stayed close to home, attending Morehead State in Kentucky—not exactly a football powerhouse.

Simms was drafted in the first round by the Giants despite the fact that he had never played a game against a top-notch college opponent. The truth is, he would have been drafted by the 49ers in the third round if the Giants hadn't taken him immediately.

Phil Simms's performance on January 25, 1987, in a jam-packed Rose Bowl was one of the greatest in Super Bowl history.

Simms got off to a wham-bang start in the NFL. He won the first five starts of his rookie year and finished with a 6–4 rookie season. He was runner-up for the 1979 NFL Rookie of the Year award. After that first year, however, things went kablooey, and Simms couldn't stay healthy. In 1980 he suffered a season-ending shoulder injury against the Redskins. In 1982 his season ended before it started when he tore up his knee against the Jets in the preseason. The Giants started the 1983 season with Scott Brunner as the starting quarterback, but he struggled. Midway through the sixth game of the year Simms was brought in to replace Brunner. Simms lasted only two drives before he hit his thumb on an opposing player's helmet while following through after a pass. Simms suffered a compound fracture that left his thumb dangling, the bone sticking up through the skin. Few who watched that game on TV will forget Simms's knees buckling as he was led off the field, a bloody towel covering his hand.

It wasn't until 1984, his fifth year with the team, that Simms emerged as a star. That year he was third in the NFL in passing yards with 4,044, and he led the Giants to the playoffs with 22 touchdown passes. The Giants were improving. They won 10 games in 1985, their most since 1963, while Simms had another great year. The highlight of the quarterback's 1985 campaign was a game against the Cincinnati Bengals in which he passed for 513 yards—a Giants best and still the fifth best ever in NFL history.

Simms's coming out of Morehead State didn't stigmatize him on this team: a group of first-round draft-pick pedigrees they were not. Jim Burt was an undrafted free agent when the Giants got him. Phil McConkey was a reclamation project working on his second, or maybe third, career. Sean Landeta, Bart Oates, and Maurice Carthon were all veterans of the United States Football League. It was a rag-tag bunch glued together into a solid unit by the coaching genius of Bill Parcells.

Guys like Harry Carson and George Martin had already been around for a while and knew even during the off-season following the 1985 season that 1986 was going to be a special season for the Giants.

Though the era of bad football continued in New York, there were intermittent reasons to smile during the '80s. The 1981 Giants—after winning only four games in 1980—made the playoffs, playing postseason football for the first time since losing their third consecutive NFL championship game in 1963. That 1981 team's defense was led

GIANTS RETIRED NUMBERS

#1	Ray Flaherty
#4	Tuffy Leemans
#7	Mel Hein
#11	Phil Simms
#14	Y.A. Tittle
#16	Frank Gifford
#32	Al Blozis
#40	Joe Morrison
#42	Charley Conerly
#50	Ken Strong
#56	Lawrence Taylor

by the "Crunch Bunch," which consisted of Harry Carson, Brad Van Pelt, Brian Kelley, and rookie Lawrence Taylor.

Taylor's addition made the Giants' defense truly frightening. At first L.T. had not been greeted with open arms by the veteran linebackers he was joining. But it didn't take him long to become accepted. Van Pelt remembered L.T. making that transition. He said, "I'll never forget it. I was pissed off because I was coming off my fifth Pro Bowl in a row, and they signed L.T. to a million-dollar bonus and the guy's making nearly twice as much as me. Then I watched him one day in practice, and I said, 'Okay, he's worth it.'"

Van Pelt also remembered that watching L.T. on film was amazing because in slow motion you could see L.T. reacting before everyone else, moving with the snap of the ball rather than just after it.

But even with L.T., the Giants floundered for a few years. Then came 1985 and another trip to the playoffs. The feeling grew that the pieces were in place and ready to jell.

THE 1986 SEASON

Years later, Carson recalled the run-up to the start of the 1986 season. He said, "When I came to minicamp I could just tell that everyone's attitude was completely different." The Giants made the 1985 playoffs but lost 21–0 to Chicago in the playoffs. That was the game when Sean Landeta tried to punt the ball out of his own end zone and missed.

Carson believes it was that loss, not any of the team's successes, that melded them into a unified unit dedicated to never losing again. And that was the feeling even at minicamp at Pace University in Pleasantville, New York, long before the season began.

Carson said, "That loss to Chicago really was the thing that galvanized us. We were just pissed that we came so close and lost. From that point on it wasn't a matter of making the playoffs because we knew we were going to make it to the playoffs. It was about winning the Super Bowl."

Carson may have felt touched by manifest destiny during camp, but Parcells, starting his fourth year as Giants coach, didn't.

"In training camp I thought for a while that we didn't have a chance," Parcells said. "There were a lot of problems early on."

Joe Morris was holding out in a contract dispute. L.T. was battling cocaine problems and had privately sought treatment. Jim Burt had a bad back. Running back George Adams was out for the season with a broken bone in his pelvis. All was not well, but Parcells was good at keeping things out of the papers; even players didn't know the full extent of their teammates' problems.

The preseason press was all positive, in fact. The NFL preview issue of *Playboy* picked the Giants to go all the way, beating the Broncos in the Super Bowl. According to the magazine's prognosticator, Anson Mount, "This will be the Year of the Giants. There are no obvious weaknesses anywhere. Quarterback Phil Simms has matured, the offensive line might be the best in the league, and the running game, with Joe Morris and George Adams, will be spectacular. Best of all is that the Giants are a stable franchise, with no internal bickering or jealousies."

After all the hype, the Giants traveled to Dallas for the opening game of the season. But they had no answer for Herschel Walker, who was making his NFL debut. Walker came in when Tony Dorsett sprained his ankle, and the Giants lost 31–28.

The following Sunday the Giants won their home opener against the San Diego Chargers. During that game, some of the pieces that would grow comfortably familiar as the season wore on fell into place. Simms passed for 300 yards. Joe Morris ran for 83. And the Chargers' Dan Fouts, who usually had his way with NFL secondaries, completed only 19 of 43 attempts versus the Giants' defense.

The next week the Giants traveled out west to meet the L.A. Raiders at the Los Angeles Coliseum. Again the Giants' defense ruled the day, holding running back Marcus Allen to 40 yards and pressuring Jim Plunkett on every pass. The Raiders managed only three field goals, while the Giants scored two touchdowns on two Simms-to-Lionel Manuel passes for the 14–9 victory. Joe Morris gained 110 yards.

The Giants proved that they had the ability to come from behind the following week. They trailed 17–0 in the second quarter to the Saints at Giants Stadium but came back to win 20–17 on two Simms touchdown passes to Zeke Mowatt and Mark Bavaro, and two field goals by Raul Allegre.

The Giants began the second quarter of the season by defeating the Cardinals in St. Louis 13–6, sacking Cards quarterback Neil Lomax seven times. Giants linebacker Carl Banks had a career game, with 10 tackles and two sacks.

The Giants' offense woke up in the Meadowlands against the Eagles the following week, blowing Philadelphia away 35–3. The most memorable touchdown of the day came on a fake field goal, when holder Jeff Rutledge threw a touchdown pass to Carson, who had lined up as a legal receiver.

That was it for the winning streak, however. The Giants traveled to the Kingdome in Seattle the following Sunday and put in a flat performance, losing to the Seahawks 17–12. Simms was sacked seven times.

Next came the key game that not many Giants fans saw. It was a Monday night game on national TV against the rival Washington Redskins, but it couldn't compete with what was on the other channel: Game Seven of the Mets–Red Sox World Series. For those of you who were watching baseball, here's what happened: the Giants pulled out to a 17-point lead, but then blew it late and had to score on the last drive of the game to win 23–20. The final touchdown came on a Joe Morris 13-yard run with 1:38 left on the clock. That night Morris had his best game of the season, gaining 181 yards on 31 rushes and 59 more yards catching the ball.

The Cowboys came to town next, and the Giants took them 17–14. Carson had 13 tackles and Morris again gained 181 yards on the ground. The Dallas passing game took a hit when Carson, who was everywhere, sacked Cowboys quarterback Danny White, breaking White's thumb.

Next up were the Eagles, to whom the Giants had administered a whomping earlier in the year. The Giants perhaps took the task too lightly and came out flat. They got things revved up for a time during the second quarter and went to the fourth quarter ahead, 17–0. Then the Giants let up again, and the Eagles came within three points of tying the score late in the game. Still, a victory is a victory, but New York knew it couldn't get away with a performance like that against a better team.

The nail-biter of the year came next. The Giants took on the Vikings at the Metrodome in Minneapolis. The teams traded field goals during the first half, with the Giants going into the break ahead 9–6. The teams then traded the lead during the second half. With time running out, the Vikings led 20–19. The Giants needed to score and found themselves at their own 48-yard line facing a fourth down and 17 yards to go—a do-or-die play if there ever was one, and the sort of play that entire seasons hinge upon. But Phil Simms, cool as a cucumber, dropped back and fired a 22-yard reception to Bobby Johnson for a first down. That fourth-down conversion may be the single most-clutch play in franchise history.

The Giants continued to move the ball, and on the final play of the game, Allegre kicked a 33-yarder for the victory, his fifth of the game. Only Joe Danelo versus Seattle in 1981 kicked more Giants field goals in a game than Allegre.

The Broncos, who were in first place in the AFC West, came to the Meadowlands next but were no match for the surging Giants. The most memorable Giants touchdown that day came when George Martin intercepted a John Elway pass and ran it back 78 yards for the score. Martin later made fun of how slowly he ran down the field. "When I caught the ball it was sunny. By the time I got to the end zone it was partly cloudy," he quipped.

Parcells had other words for the moment. "That was the greatest play I've ever seen," the coach said of Martin's touchdown.

Next came the 49ers, with the Giants playing their third Monday night game of the season. During the first half, the 49ers defense held Morris to 14 yards on the ground on 13 attempts, and San Francisco had a solid lead at the half. However, the tide turned completely in the third quarter. Whatever Parcells said to his team during the break sure worked. Simms threw two touchdown passes to Robinson and Morris, and Ottis Anderson added another touchdown on the ground, giving Big Blue a 21–17 win.

Next up on the schedule were the Redskins. Both New York and Washington had 11–2 records, but once again the Giants' defense was devastating. Redskins quarterback Jay Schroeder was forced to pass the ball 51 times, and the Giants' defense picked off five of them. The Giants won 24–14 and were all alone atop the NFC East.

The Giants finished the season with routs over the lesser Cardinals and Packers and soared into the playoffs.

The stats for the regular season showed why the team had been so hard to beat. Morris gained 1,516 yards. Simms passed for 3,487, and Bavaro had more than 1,000 yards receiving—pretty amazing considering he played six weeks with his broken jaw wired shut, eating all his food through a straw. And L.T. led the NFL in sacks with 20.5.

Burt later recalled, "We were a juggernaut by the end of the season. No one could touch us."

Leonard Marshall remembered that the team grew confident on and off the field: "There were different guys in the locker room, all very youthful, full of piss and vinegar, just coming together for one cause. New York hadn't had a football team to identify with for almost 30 years. And then this group comes along and puts New York on its back and says, 'I'm gonna carry New York every time I walk out the door. I'm gonna carry the attitude. I'm gonna carry the toughness. I'm gonna carry the resilience it takes to be identified as a champion.'"

McConkey recalled, "It was a bunch of guys that just wanted to know when and where. If you told that team the game was at midnight on the Brooklyn Bridge against the Jersey City Destroyers, those guys would show up and play hard."

Bavaro, a man of few words even when his jaw wasn't wired shut, later said, "Parcells called us lunch-pail guys. I didn't understand it, but looking at the players today, absolutely."

Burt called it a "blue-collar situation." Burt remembered, "Even L.T., as great as he was, wasn't a flashy guy. We never took the pads off. We would grind on people. We did it the grinding, grinding, grinding way. And you know what, that goes for the quarterback, too."

THE PLAYOFFS

The most memorable playoff victory on the road to the Super Bowl for the Giants was over the 49ers at Giants Stadium on January 4, 1987, in the NFC divisional round. In that game Simms threw four touchdown passes—to Bavaro, Johnson, McConkey, and Mowatt.

The stifling Giants defense held San Francisco's running game to a measly 29 yards for the day. And L.T. built his legend before our very eyes.

The Giants probably had their all-time greatest defense that year. They were known as the "Big Blue Wrecking Crew." And Taylor was the greatest of the greats. He dominated the league at outside linebacker. He changed the way teams ran their offense. Joe Gibbs, the coach of the Redskins, admitted that he devised the two-tight-end offense as a way to prevent L.T. from getting to Redskins quarterbacks unhindered whenever the Giants blitzed.

The other Giants linebackers were Banks and Carson, legends themselves. But L.T. was the man. That year, L.T. became one of only four defensive players ever to be named NFL MVP. Before his career was through, he'd play in 10 Pro Bowls and be elected Defensive Player of the Year three times.

The Giants' ultimate victory over the San Francisco 49ers was partly caused by a really good Giants team. But it was also partly caused by the 49ers, who were making inexplicable unforced errors. Jerry Rice, the 49ers future Hall of Fame wide receiver, was on his way to a 50-yard touchdown catch, running with the greatest of ease, when out of nowhere the football squirted loose. Of course, the Giants recovered it, then marched 80 yards down the field to score on a 24-yard touchdown pass from Simms to Bavaro. And the 49ers probably could have gotten on their team bus right then and there.

The 49ers' Joe Montana, truly one of the great quarterbacks in the history of the game, threw an interception to Taylor, who ran 34 yards for the touchdown. That turned out to be Montana's last play of the season, as he was knocked out cold soon thereafter by Burt.

One of the reasons Burt is so popular in New York to this very day is that once upon a time, back when Giants walked the earth, he gave Montana a little snooze on the hard carpet of combat. Montana had fewer than one hundred yards passing before his how-many-fingers exit. His replacement, Jeff Kemp, only passed for 64 yards. That was the extent of the 49ers' offensive output.

Afterward, Coach Parcells said, "It wasn't a perfect game—but it was close."

One week later the Giants met the Washington Redskins in the NFC Championship Game to decide who would go to the Super Bowl. They say it is hard to beat the same football team twice in the same season, but that was what the Giants had done to the Redskins. The odds of beating the same team three times in a season were also harsh, so said the experts. The Redskins had made it into the conference-championship round by beating the Rams and the Bears.

Parcells didn't think the Redskins were going to be a pushover despite the Giants' past successes. He told his team that the Redskins were still the most dangerous team they had faced all season. The psyche of football success, Parcells felt, had very little to do with over-confidence and everything to do with fear of defeat, embarrassment, and humiliation.

A record crowd of 76,633 at Giants Stadium watched on January 11, 1987, as the Redskins came to town. In true Giants postseason tradition, the weather was miserable. It was cold, and the wind was gusting up to 35 miles per hour. Kicking the football was going to be hard no matter which direction you were headed. The wind swirled in the Giants Stadium bowl, and footballs can do strange things in gusts like that. Passing would be difficult, too. The team that could most depend on its ground game was going to advance to the Super Bowl. Behind Morris, the Giants were that team, and the Redskins failed to score a point all day.

Despite the gusting wind, Parcells sent Allegre out in the first quarter to attempt a 47-yard field goal. Allegre waited until a gust died down and nailed the field goal. By the second half, the Redskins had given up on their futile ground game. Washington quarterback Schroeder passed 50 times and ran the ball once. That didn't get it done.

Even when the Redskins had opportunities to score, they couldn't execute. During the second quarter, Schroeder threw a bomb that hit normally sure-handed receiver Gary Clark right in the mitts for what appeared to be a sure touchdown, but—clang—the ball bounced off and fell incomplete.

The Giants led 17–0 at halftime, and the second half was scoreless. Big Blue had completely dominated the Redskins and was on its way to sunshiny Pasadena, California, to play the Denver Broncos in Super Bowl XXI.

ROSE BOWL REMINISCIN'

Giants offensive lineman Brad Benson, who went to his only Pro Bowl that year, remembered the flight from Newark Airport to Los Angeles. He said, "You knew the plane trip from Newark to California was something special because everybody on the plane had Betamaxes or VHSes. The guys were interviewing one another on their thoughts on the Super Bowl. Bill Parcells had our pilot flown from California to New York to fly us to California because he had flown two previous Super Bowl winners. There were a lot of fans at the airport when we left, and even the policemen were getting autographs. And when we landed in California, a lot of fans were waiting for us. It's nice to get support like that. We're not oblivious to it."

Keeping a football team focused during the week before a Super Bowl can be hard. Press interest skyrockets, and the host city usually throws a weeklong party that spills into the streets and makes hotels noisy at night. Under those conditions, it can be a little tough to keep a group of men tucked in their beds getting their beauty sleep.

As soon as the Giants got to California, Parcells called a practice, and he was tough on his team. He made them work, and he made them think. That set the tone. Parcells kept their minds on football by working them hard.

A lot of the Giants, including Benson, thought concentrating on football was the easiest way to relax. It was the Super Bowl hoopla that was stressful. A lot of the players just weren't prepared for it. They lacked the social skills to be a star guest at a big party. (Well, some could handle it; L.T. probably excelled at it.) Benson remembered: "With all those calls I was getting, it was nice getting away. You don't want to be rude to anybody, but if I returned every phone call, I wouldn't have time to go to practice or else I wouldn't have time to sleep at night. For example, I got a call from a guy I met once, a friend of a girl I went to high school with. There were 3,000 people in high school, and I didn't know her that well. This guy lives in California, and he wanted to have me over for dinner. You can't be angry with someone who extends himself like that, but there are so many people."

On the morning of Super Bowl XXI, Father Moore said mass for the players, but he ended up cutting the ceremony short because a lot of the players were too fidgety. They ate their pregame meal together at the hotel. Most of them took taxis from the hotel to the stadium.

The 65-year-old Rose Bowl, which was to be the site of the Super Bowl for the fourth time, not only held more than 100,000 people, but was in an idyllic setting, resting in a dry riverbed called Arroyo Seco along the foot of the Linda Vista Hills, with the San Gabriel Mountains in the distance.

From the minute he arrived at the Rose Bowl, Phil Simms had a grin on his face and wouldn't shut up. He said, "I feel real good. I'm throwing fastballs today, guys. I'm telling you, I feel great."

At kickoff, Las Vegas oddsmakers had the Giants as nine-and-a-half-point favorites despite the million-dollar arm of Denver quarterback John Elway. And it looked like Elway was heading toward an MVP performance in the first quarter. He completed his first six passes crisply. The Broncos scored first, when Rich Karlis kicked a 48-yard field goal little more than four minutes into the first quarter. At the time, Karlis's boot tied the Super Bowl record for longest field goal ever.

The Giants and Broncos then traded long drives and touchdowns. Simms successfully completed a nine-play drive when he

HARRY CARSON

Harry Carson, who played 13 years for the Giants, saw a whole lot of everything. He was the team leader, the guy his teammates were most willing to march into battle with. He was the official captain of the Giants for his last 10 campaigns. He was a key member of the defense that led Big Blue to its Super Bowl XXI victory. Carson was named to the All-Rookie team after his first year, and by the time he was finished, he was ranked as the all-time number-one inside linebacker in NFL history by *Pro Football Weekly* magazine. He played in nine Pro Bowls. He was named All-NFL seven times, All-NFC eight times, and the NFC Linebacker of the Year twice. He loved the spotlight and had his greatest game on *Monday Night Football*.

His greatest game? Hell, it was one of the greatest games ever played by a football player on either side of the ball. Against the Green Bay Packers, Carson made an incredible 25 tackles.

Carson grew up in Florence, South Carolina, where he attended Wilson Senior High and McClenaghan High Schools. Showing leadership qualities from the start, he was a class president and ROTC commander. He earned a BS degree in education at South Carolina State University.

He was captain of the university's football team during his junior and senior years. As a Bulldog he played on the defensive line, collecting 114 tackles and 17 sacks as a senior. He made the Kodak All-American Football Team, the NAIA All-American Team, and the *Pittsburgh Courier* All-American Team. He was named All-State (South Carolina), All Mid-Eastern Athletic Conference, and was MEAC Defensive Player of the Year twice. Gifted in the classroom as well, one year he had the highest academic average among Black College All-Americans.

Since his retirement from football in 1988, he has worked as a broadcaster. He is also a successful businessman. He is CEO of Harry Carson, Inc., a sports consulting and promotions company. The company pairs former professional athletes with schools and corporations to deliver motivational and inspirational speeches.

Carson has written two books: *Point of Attack* and *The Smell of Freshly Cut Grass*. He has done much charity work and is a member of at least 10 halls of fame, including the College Football Hall of Fame and the Pro Football Hall of Fame. His hobbies include playing golf, bass fishing, auto racing, and target shooting.

Harry Carson, who turned 33 during the 1986 season, said after winning the Super Bowl, "This has been a long time coming, I just wish I didn't have to wait so long." (Photo courtesy of Getty Images)

threw a six-yard touchdown pass to Mowatt, and Elway returned the favor by culminating a six-play drive with a quarterback draw for a four-yard touchdown.

A big momentum-turner came when the Giants executed a goal-line stand at the start of the second quarter. The Broncos drove down the field all the way to the Giants' 1, with first and goal to go.

The Broncos ran three consecutive running plays and were unable to punch the ball into the end zone. Playing conservatively, Denver's coach Dan Reeves sent place-kicker Karlis onto the field, but Karlis missed the point-blank field goal. What should have been seven points had dissolved into zero, and it would be a while before the Broncos' offense got back on track.

The only scoring in the second quarter came when George Martin sacked Elway in the end zone for a safety with just under three minutes left in the half. The score at halftime was 10–9 Denver.

"We came in with a slight advantage at halftime," said Bill Bryan, the Broncos' center, after the game. "And it just evaporated in the third quarter, like Dr. Jekyll and Mr. Hyde."

The third quarter was indeed all Giants. They had proven earlier in the season, against the 49ers for example, that they could score points in a hurry. That was what they did in the Super Bowl, when it mattered most.

Simms threw his second touchdown pass of the day, this one to tight end Bavaro for 13 yards. A 21-yard field goal by Allegre and a one-yard touchdown run by Morris gave the Giants a 26–10 lead. The Giants scored the first four times they had the ball in the second half.

In the meantime, the Giants' defense—led by Banks, Carson, Leonard Marshall, and Taylor—which had been stifling to opponents all year, shut down the Broncos' offense. By the time the Broncos scored again, the Giants had a huge lead.

One of the reasons the game blew open in the second half was that Parcells called a couple of trick plays, and they worked. There's no bigger gamble for a coach than to attempt a trick play in a big game. If it works it can give a team the momentum necessary for victory. But—and it's a huge but—a trick play that gets stopped can kill a team's momentum, sometimes irreparably. On the fourth play of the third quarter, the Giants were on their 46-yard line, with fourth down and a foot to go. In came punter Landeta, as well as backup quarterback Rutledge, not a usual member of the punting team. Rutledge lined up in a blocking-back position, but just before the ball was snapped, he jumped behind center to take the snap. He sneaked for two yards and the first down. Five plays later, Simms found Bavaro for the touchdown, and the Giants had the lead for good.

"Jeff [Rutledge] could take a delay or run," said Parcells after the game about that fake punt. "He looked over at me, I nodded my head, and he went for it. We went for it because we're trying to win the game. This is for the world championship. I have a lot of confidence in our guys."

The other trick play came late in the third quarter. The Giants were on the Broncos' 45-yard line. Simms took the center snap and handed the ball to Morris, who ran a couple of steps, stopped, and threw the ball back to Simms. The flea flicker! Simms passed to a wide-open McConkey, who caught the ball at the 20 and ran to the Broncos' 1. Morris scored on the next play.

"We've run the flea flicker in practice for I don't know how long," said Simms, "and we've never hit on the damn thing. When I hit McConkey down on the 1, I thought, 'That's it. We've won it.'"

In the fourth quarter Simms connected again, this time in one of the game's most memorable plays. Simms threw the ball to Bavaro, but the pass bounced off the intended receiver's usually reliable hands and happily into the waiting arms of McConkey in the back of the end zone for a six-yard touchdown pass.

In a span of 15 minutes and four seconds that covered parts of the third and fourth quarters, the Giants scored 24 points. In the process, Simms threw a Super Bowl–record 10 consecutive completions. The machine was as well-oiled as any ever to take the gridiron.

The Broncos responded with a 28-yard Karlis field goal. Then Ottis Anderson scored a two-yard Giants touchdown with a little more than three minutes left in the game. The Broncos returned fire a minute later on a 47-yard pass from Elway to Vance Johnson—but it was too little too late, and the Giants won 39–20.

The Giants had a substantial advantage on the scoreboard but not that big of an advantage in the statistics. The Broncos had gained 372 yards during the game, and the Giants 399. The Broncos earned 23 first downs, and the Giants only one more than that.

Naturally, Simms was named MVP. He had been deadly accurate throughout the game, and one of the reasons for his success was that he equally distributed his passes among all of his pass receivers. Bavaro, Morris, and Carthon each caught four passes. Stacy Robinson and Manuel caught three apiece, and three other receivers split the other four completions. Mowatt's touchdown catch was his only reception of the game.

Although Morris had carried the ball 20 times, he hadn't been particularly effective, but he didn't have to be, not with Simms routinely extending drives by converting third downs through the air.

Morris's ball-carrying, in addition to gaining a little more than 60 yards over the course of the game, also served to keep the clock running. That's one of Parcells's theories of victory—when you are ahead, you have to get to the end of the game as quickly as possible. You have to keep the clock rolling, and that means running the football and completing passes up the middle—something the Giants did again and again throughout their magic day.

The Giants' emphasis on the pass caught the Broncos by surprise. They had geared themselves up to stop Morris, thinking that if they put a halt to the Giants' ground game Simms wouldn't have the stuff to win the game on his own. It didn't turn out that way.

"I was surprised they changed their whole offensive attack," said Karl Mecklenburg, the Broncos' inside linebacker. "Pass first, run second—it surprised us. We thought they would try to establish the running game, but they went against their tendencies and did a good job of it."

The Giants set the record for most points scored in one half of a Super Bowl with their 30-point second-half output.

When it was over and Carson had doused Parcells with the Gatorade, Burt and McConkey ran up into the Rose Bowl stands to get up close to their fans and to visit their families. Burt carried his son back onto the field.

Pepper Johnson and William Roberts danced on the 50-yard line. Chris Godfrey and Benson carried Parcells on their shoulders. Making a crack about Parcells's weight, Godfrey later said, "I was thinking, 'God, when am I going to be able to let this guy down?' I was extremely happy to be with him, close to him at that moment. He's my coach, but he's also my friend."

The Super Bowl victory over the Broncos had been the Giants' 12th straight win, with nine in the regular season and three in the postseason.

Parcells and 70-year-old team owner Wellington Mara joined NFL commissioner Pete Rozelle in the Giants locker room for the presentation of the Vince Lombardi Trophy. Rozelle handed the trophy to Mara, who handed the trophy to Parcells. The Giants were the NFL champions for the first time in 30 years.

"In my wildest dreams," said Simms after the game, "I couldn't have hoped it would work out this way."

"That's as good as Phil has ever played," said Parcells. "This dispelled for the last time any myth about Phil Simms. He was absolutely magnificent today."

Parcells himself was vindicated to a certain degree. His first year with the team, 1983, had been a disaster. The Giants had managed only three victories, and Parcells almost lost his job. But the team had made the playoff all three years since then, and now they were on top of the football world.

After the game, the Giants received a call from President Reagan, inviting them to have breakfast at the White House, a tradition for the Super Bowl victors.

The Giants finished the postseason with a cumulative score of 105–23. And before the Super Bowl, they had accomplished routs against the 49ers, 49–3, and the Washington Redskins, 17–0.

"Now," said Taylor, "no matter what people say about our team, whether the Giants don't look good anymore or whatever, as long as I live, I'll always have a Super Bowl ring. One time in my career, we are considered the best in the world. That was the most important thing."

"This has been a long time coming," added Carson. "I just wish I didn't have to wait so long." As it turned out, the Rose Bowl victory was Carson's only Super Bowl. Carson only played two more seasons after that for the Giants, giving him a grand total of 13 seasons in New York. By the time the Giants returned to the Super Bowl, Carson was retired.

"It was great," said Wellington Mara, one of the few men around who had attended every one of the Giants' previous NFL championship victories (1934, 1938, 1956). "But I tried to be professional about it and remember it was great to win our other championships, too. To the people on the inside of the organization, it's just as big as it was back then. But there's more outside pressures now that you try to shield the players from."

Mara watched the game with some Giants alumni who had been around for the previous victories. Mara said, "Charley Conerly told me, 'I was so into that game, I was so excited.' And Ken Kavanaugh, who coached the receivers on that 1956 team, asked me, 'Where is Simms? I've got to tell him how great he was.'

"Conerly and Y.A. Tittle had big games for us," Mara continued, "but maybe not in that big a game. I wouldn't trade Simms for any quarterback in the game. For our team, in our environment, he's the perfect quarterback. He's tough; maybe strong is the better word. He's strong mentally, physically, and spiritually."

And what did Parcells say to his team before the game?

"I told them," Parcells recalled, "'Don't tell me that the Super Bowl guarantees that you'll play hard. I've seen some teams that didn't play hard in the Super Bowl, so play hard.'"

After the game Simms got to be the hero, and Broncos placekicker Karlis got to be the goat. Videotaped interviews with Karlis after the game show his eyes red-rimmed, swollen, and moist with tears. He'd missed two field-goal attempts, one from extra-point distance. Indeed, it was the chippy that seemed to have changed the game, turning a possible victory into a sure defeat. Denver was going to need someone to hate, and Karlis, both of whose misses were wide right, was pretty sure it was going to be him.

"I hurt our momentum," Karlis said. "The snap was good, the hold was good, everything was good. I feel like I let everybody down." The fact that he had tied a Super Bowl record with a 48-yarder was forgotten. "We didn't want to waste many opportunities today, but I did. I really felt I had answered all of my critics this year. I made some big kicks. I had a big year. But this leaves a sour note."

The day after the victory the press conferences just kept coming. Parcells was starting to look a little haggard, although happy. Simms looked as fresh as a daisy. He was ready for nothing but press conferences and maybe a trip to Disney World, forever and ever.

They were the only two people left to face the press. Everyone else from the Giants was through answering questions. Maybe the party was still going on somewhere—and we mean you, L.T.—but most of the press was gone. Now Parcells and Simms were a duo, and Simms was the only one who could be correctly described as chipper.

Parcells said, "It's pretty difficult for me to describe how I felt yesterday. I think I know what real euphoria is. It's absolutely wonderful. I don't know if you can ever duplicate this feeling. I sure hope so; it was terrific."

Perhaps realizing his and his teammates' careers had changed forever, Simms added, "In years to come...I won the Super Bowl. We won the Super Bowl, the Giants. They can't take that away from us."

Again it was the coach's turn. Parcells said, "With a minute to go, really, honest, I don't want this to sound dramatic or anything, but I thought back to the first game I ever coached, at Hastings College in 1964. It is all relative. It's just as important to you at the time."

Turning to the game itself, a reporter asked the quarterback if he was aware that, of the 11 first downs the Giants earned in the first half, he threw for nine of them.

Simms said, "I knew we were going to start out being aggressive, trying to throw the ball. I didn't want to run, run, get to third-and-10 and ask me to get 10 yards, do it again and get eight, then wonder why we're not in the game in the first quarter. I wanted a chance to be a factor in the game. I thought that was important."

Simms said it came as no shock to him that he played as well as he had: "I kind of felt that way all week. I was throwing the ball in practice as well as I could have. Before the game, I commented to a couple of players that I felt like I could put it in there where I wanted."

How about that defense, Coach?

"Unbridled," Parcells said. "They were just running around wild, making a few plays but not very many. We started to settle down after that."

It had been a one-point game at halftime, so the coach was asked what he said to his players at halftime.

"We have to play with a little more discipline. You're going to give it away; let's not go out there and get beat," Parcells answered.

Coach Parcells thought the flea flicker was the key play in the game.

"When we hit the flea flicker, we really had a tremendous volume of momentum," Parcells said. "We were dominating the third quarter pretty well. Once we hit that one and got the touchdown, I knew we would be hard to beat."

Will the Giants be back?

"If we get some more good players and we come back with a renewed attitude. Upgrade the program. Get more good players. Collect as many good players as you can. That's the whole idea in this business," Parcells said.

VICTORY CELEBRATION

It was the Tuesday morning after Super Bowl Sunday, and the location was Giants Stadium, where the frigid tailgating had commenced in the parking lot at 8:30 AM. Later that morning, fans were let into the stadium, and each was issued a complimentary kazoo as he or she passed the turnstile. The first 8,000 fans were allowed to stay on the field, and the rest went up into the stands.

A few days prior there had been a blizzard in New York, and soon huge chunks of snow were being thrown by fans with one hand as they held their kazoos to their lips with the other.

Some New Jersey firefighters had shown up, and they hoped to raise their ladders and drop confetti on the players when they eventually paraded around the stadium. Normally New York sports teams that win it all are given ticker-tape parades down Broadway in the financial district. But these Giants weren't going to get that. The franchise had pulled up its roots at Shea Stadium in Queens and had moved to New Jersey. No ticker-tape parade in the Garden State. So the firefighters, from the Moonachie Fire Department, had hoped to give the deprived players some of that

SUPER BOWL XXI

Rose Bowl, Pasadena, California, January 25, 1987

	1	2	3	4	Total
Broncos	10	0	0	10	20
Giants	7	2	17	13	39

Attendance: 101,063

ticker-tape feel, but Giants management refused to allow the truck to enter the stadium.

Everyone had a kazoo and knew how to use it. Now, if the crowd could have gotten it together to do, in unison, Clarence Clemons's sax solo from "Born to Run," that would have been one thing. But disorganization was king, and the kazoos made the celebration sound a bit like a combination of Times Square when the ball drops and a nine-year-old's sugared-up birthday party.

Before the Giants made their appearance, there were some warm-up acts. Captain Lou Albano, the former pro wrestler, spewed some pseudo-motivational nonsense.

Professor Irwin Corey, a comedian whose whole shtick was that he spoke a river of gibberish while proclaiming himself, without qualification "the world's greatest authority," did five minutes that seemed like a half hour.

After Irwin Corey was booed off the stage, the event organizers played "Beer-Barrel Polka" over the public-address system, and there was an immediate cacophony of kazoos that couldn't have been more out of sync with the music playing.

Tiny Tim sang "Tiptoe through the Tulips." Henny Youngman came out and said, "Take my wife. Please." Joe Piscopo and David Brenner did some lame standup. It almost seemed designed to disappoint.

The fans pelted the performers with what were euphemistically called snowballs, but were actually rock-hard ice chunks. The temperature was 13 degrees. Not even all of the Giants were there, although some of them had a good excuse, being on a plane to Hawaii where they had to play in the Pro Bowl.

When the once-around-the-park parade was complete, the players, Parcells, and his staff were deposited beside the stage.

It was probably the only victory celebration in a franchise's history during which the city in the team's name was routinely booed. If anyone said "New York," they were booed and hissed by the New Jersey natives.

Yes, vociferously. And with gusto.

If someone said "New Jersey," as in "New Jersey Giants," they were cheered wildly. There was way too much security—made up of all sorts of cops, as well as National Guardsmen—but those charged with keeping the peace relaxed once they saw that the crowd was too cold to be violent or angry. As long as no one got hit in the face with an ice ball (and no one did), everything was cool. First-aid attendants treated one guy who got himself punched in the nose, but otherwise, organizers didn't have much to do.

Up on stage, Governor Thomas H. Kean of New Jersey gave the players gold medallions. Coach Parcells made a short speech. He knew a cold crowd when he saw one. A marching band played, and highlights of the season were shown on the scoreboard.

Later that day, New York City Mayor Ed Koch said that he had reconsidered, and he did think it was appropriate for the Giants to get a real ticker-tape parade after all. "The Giants can have two parades," the mayor said. "One a practice parade in the Meadowlands, a walk around the stadium, and the second a ticker-tape parade down Broadway."

Koch cited his "regional pride" when he made his statement.

The Giants, Jersey all the way, said no thanks.

Who paid for the Jersey party at the Meadowlands? Apparently it was some rich guys who preferred to remain anonymous. According to a New Jersey Sports and Exposition Authority spokesman named Paul Wolcott, $650,000 had been raised through private donations. Very good.

On the 20th anniversary of the Giants' first Super Bowl victory, reporters from all of New York's papers called various Giants from

WHERE ARE THEY TODAY?

A lot of the 1986 Giants have done big things with their post-football lives. Raul Allegre does Spanish play-by-play for NFL games. Ottis Anderson is the president of O.J. Anderson Enterprises. Carl Banks has his own clothing line and is a color commentator on Giants radio broadcasts. Mark Bavaro is a financial consultant. Brad Benson owns the Brad Benson Auto Group. Jim Burt owns an indoor-sports facility with his son. Harry Carson is CEO of Harry Carson, Inc. Maurice Carthon is the running-back coach for the Arizona Cardinals. Chris Godfrey is an attorney. Pepper Johnson is the defensive-line coach for the Patriots. Lionel Manuel is a chef. Leonard Marshall is a financial planner. George Martin is a financial adviser. Phil McConkey is a money manager. Bart Oates is a lawyer. Jerome Sally is an assistant principal at a Missouri high school and a color commentator on Mizzou radio broadcasts. Phil Simms is the lead football analyst for CBS Sports, and Perry Williams is a professor at Fairleigh Dickenson University.

the 1986 team. To a man, they said that the feelings of victory and camaraderie had never left them.

"I only played with the Giants for four years, and compared to the 20 years that passed, it only seems like a drop in the bucket," said right guard Godfrey. "But we go through life together in a sense, and it's because we had those strong relationships forged together. That moment, frozen in time 20 years ago, has cemented us all."

Banks said, "We won a lot of games and we won another Super Bowl, but that [first] Super Bowl sealed a lifetime bond with a family of teammates. It was one of those teams where one man's fight was every man's fight."

McConkey said, "Harry Carson and George Martin will be my captains forever."

Today Parcells says of those players, "They were resilient, like all championship teams, mentally tough. They knew how to play, and they were physically dominant. I sure am proud of them, and indebted to them, as well. The thing I'm most proud of is the widespread success that a lot of the kids have had in their personal lives going forward. The team was pretty achievement-oriented. It was a pretty special group of guys. It was like a blood kinship."

Simms's post-football career has been extremely successful. His reputation for being "practically perfect" persists. In 1995 Simms became NBC's lead football analyst and served as a third of that network's premiere broadcast team, with Dick Enberg and Paul Maguire. He joined CBS Sports in January 1998 as lead analyst for their NFL coverage. Simms and Greg Gumbel were paired as the network's lead NFL announcer team. The first Super Bowl Simms analyzed was XXX. His skills haven't been limited to just football announcing, either. He announced weight-lifting events for NBC Sports's coverage of the 1996 Summer Olympics in Atlanta, and was a sideline reporter on the *NBA on NBC*. In addition to his broadcasting duties, Simms gives motivational speeches called "Winning in the NFL and Winning in Life." Simms still holds the team's records for most passes completed and attempted for one game (40 completed, 62 attempted), one season (286, 533), and career (2576, 4647); career touchdown passes (199); and most 300-yard games in a career (21).

THE BAD

That's enough highlights. Time for some lowlights. It makes me remember the Giants' slogan from the early 1980s: "Because we love the pain!"

THE 1993 PLAYOFF DISASTER

The great Giants teams of the '80s and early '90s couldn't last forever. If you want to pick a single moment when that era died, pick the game in San Francisco's Candlestick Park during the divisional round of the 1993 playoffs. The Giants suddenly looked done, outmatched by the vastly superior 49ers.

Not only did the Giants get outplayed in every way, but Lawrence Taylor announced his retirement in the locker room after the game. Five months later, the Giants released Phil Simms. The glory days were over.

The 49ers made the Giants look like a team that no longer even belonged in the playoffs. San Francisco scored the first three times it had the ball and led 16–0. The score was 23–3 at halftime, and things never got any better.

Ricky Watters of the 49ers set a record that day, running for five touchdowns. All came on runs six yards and shorter. The Giants' rushing attack was held to just 41 yards all day. And Simms looked like a quarterback on his last legs, which he was.

1993 NFC DIVISIONAL PLAYOFF GAME

Candlestick Park, San Francisco, California, January 15, 1994

	1	2	3	4	Total
Giants	0	3	0	0	3
49ers	9	14	14	7	44

Attendance: 67,143

Simms's retirement began the oft-forgotten Dave Brown era. For three and a half years Brown was the Giants' starting quarterback, sporting a quarterback rating that never rose above the low 70s. At first they talked about Brown's potential. Then they talked about his inconsistency. Then they tried to unload him, finally accomplishing that feat. After leaving the Giants, Brown played parts of four seasons with the Cards before calling it a disappointing career.

THE 1997 NFC WILD-CARD GAME

Teams usually can't get it together to play as a single unit to defeat another qualified NFL team if they are fighting amongst themselves. And, judging from the scuffling and yapping, there was a lot of fighting going on along the Giants' sideline in Giants Stadium on December 27, 1997, for the wild-card game versus the Minnesota Vikings.

During the game, this Giants team didn't get along very well at all. And, sure enough, it lost its focus and, in the end, lost the game.

The Giants were ahead by 16 points at halftime, taking advantage of three Randall Cunningham turnovers. In the second half the Giants came out fighting amongst themselves and, in the process, lost the battle with the Vikings. The offense stopped clicking, and the defense stopped altogether. The second-half collapse

The 1993 playoffs meant the end of an era for the Giants, as Lawrence Taylor (top) retired moments after a loss to the 49ers, and Phil Simms (bottom) was released five months later.

1997 NFC WILD-CARD GAME

Giants Stadium, East Rutherford, New Jersey, December 27, 1997

	1	2	3	4	Total
Vikings	0	3	7	13	23
Giants	6	13	0	3	22

Attendance: 77,710

started out with a small crack, then everything fell apart in the last minute. Make that the last minute and a half. With 90 seconds left in the game, the Giants were still ahead by nine points. Then the walls really did cave in. The Vikings pulled to within two points when Cunningham hit Jake Reed for a 30-yard touchdown pass. The Vikings tried an onside kick and recovered it when the Giants' Chris Calloway muffed it. The Vikings then kicked a field goal in the last second to win the game by one point.

The Giants, already a team divided, stood motionless with a "what happened?" expression on their collective faces. What did happen? For one thing, the Giants' ground game had stunk up the joint. A young Tiki Barber carried the ball 17 times for only 29 yards. Rodney Hampton, a Texas kid out of the University of Georgia, ran eight times for 18 yards. Barber was the new guy coming in and Hampton was the old guy going out, and on that day, neither one of them got it done. It was Hampton's last game in the NFL, the end of an eight-season career, all with the Giants. During those eight seasons, Rodney had been a leader on offense, gaining better than 1,000 yards in five consecutive seasons.

THE UGLY

O h, and we do mean ugly. Snap, crackle, pop. The only consolation is that Joe Theismann's career was pretty much over anyway.

JOE THEISMANN'S LEG

It was a Monday night. Everybody remembers that part. November 18, 1985. Giants versus Redskins. That was the night that Joe Theismann's name became synonymous with *ewwwwwwww*. That is, he became synonymous with a gruesome injury. The injury that made Lawrence Taylor cry.

Joe Theismann later recalled the night of his injury vividly. He had gone into what turned out to be the last game of his career with a great sense of optimism. The Redskins hadn't been playing well, and neither had he. But he saw the big game on national TV against the archrival Giants as the perfect opportunity to get his game and the team back on track.

Theismann hadn't looked good lately. It had been, by far, the worst of his 12 years with the Redskins. He was originally from New Jersey and had played football at Notre Dame, where the pronunciation of his last name was changed so that it would rhyme with Heisman. It was originally pronounced *Thees*-man.

Theismann had a great career at Notre Dame but never won the trophy. He had to start his pro career in Canada because at an

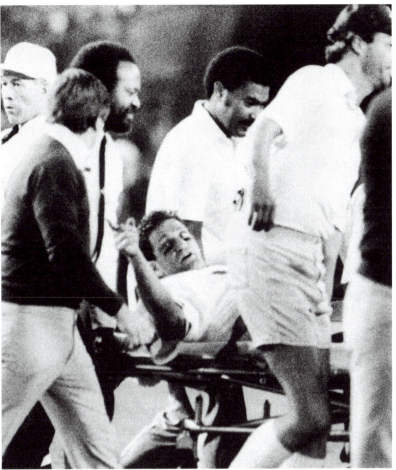

By the time Joe Theismann was taken off the field after his horrific injury, most of America had been traumatized.

even 6'0", he was considered too short to play quarterback in the NFL. He made his NFL debut in 1974 and was still going strong 12 seasons later. During those years he had started a Redskins-record 71 consecutive games and won a Super Bowl ring. He is still the Redskins' all-time leading passer with 25,206 yards. But the thing everyone remembers about him is the final play of his career.

Sometimes Theismann talked about that night. Not much, but sometimes. Theismann remembered that he'd had a strong first quarter, completing 70 percent of his passes, and that it was the beginning of the second quarter when it happened.

Up until then the game had been close and hard-fought. The Redskins took the lead in the first quarter with a 10-yard touchdown pass from Theismann to tight end Don Warren. The Giants tied the game on a 56-yard run from scrimmage by Joe Morris.

The second quarter had just begun. Washington had a first down at their own 46. Head coach Joe Gibbs called the next play: "Fifty-gut throwback." More commonly known as a flea flicker. Theismann took the snap and handed off to running back John Riggins. Riggins took a couple of steps, stopped, and then turned to toss the ball back to Theismann, who would look to hit one of his receivers downfield.

But right away things started to go wrong for the Redskins. Giants linebacker Harry Carson pushed his way through the Redskins offensive line, and, by the time Theismann received Riggins's pitch, the quarterback was no longer alone in the pocket—Carson was there with him. So Theismann had to scramble. The pocket ended up collapsing on him from all sides, and Lawrence Taylor, the greatest linebacker ever, got to his target after circling around from the rear. As Theismann planted his back leg to throw, L.T. came down hard on his lower leg. Both bones in Theismann's lower leg, the tibia and fibula, simultaneously snapped like a pair of toothpicks. The bones stuck out through Theismann's skin and through his sock. His body folded and then collapsed. He started to scream in agony. He lifted his helmet to look at his lower leg, which appeared detached and pointed outward at a grotesque angle.

L.T., the perceived killer, saw the damage that had been done and burst into tears—big tears that flowed down his face. He turned and began to wave with panicky gestures. Serious medical attention was needed. Stat.

Giants legend Frank Gifford was calling the play-by-play on ABC's *Monday Night Football*:

First and 10, Riggins, flea flicker back to Theismann. Theismann's in a lot of trouble. And it was Lawrence

Taylor who slammed Theismann to the ground at the 42-yard line. The blitz was on, that's not necessarily a good play to have called, and quickly Lawrence Taylor is up, saying Theismann is hurt. And I don't believe Lawrence Taylor would have reacted that way unless Theismann is really hurt. He slammed him to the natural surface here. The blitz was on. That is not a good play to have with the blitz on. Theismann has no chance at all to get downfield, and let's take one more look at it with our reverse-angle camera. He's looking deep, and he knows he's in trouble. Lawrence Taylor, number 56, right there. Carson is number 53. But it's Taylor, over Carson—ooh—and you can see the uh, right knee, the right foot. And I knew that something was really bad. And Lawrence Taylor leaped to his feet and beckoned over to the Redskins bench: get your medical team in here quickly.

ABC cameraman Jack Cronin was trying to communicate to the production truck that they might want to think twice about airing his instant-replay footage. He knew he had the best angle, and he knew it was horrible. But the order not to show the replay was never given. The director, Chet Forte, saw the replay before it aired. The only warning he gave his broadcast team was, "Guys, this is ugly."

Theismann later told sports writer Thom Loverro, "The moment that my leg was broken, you could say that changed my life completely. I had become very egocentric. The only thing that mattered to me was being a football star. Even though I had lots of material things, as a person, I was probably as low as you could get."

He remembered all of the movements in the pocket during the fateful flea flicker. Theismann later recalled, "I remember handing the ball to John, getting it back, and then looking downfield. I couldn't find Art Monk deep, and then I looked to my right for tight end Donnie Warren. At that point, I was feeling some pressure."

He remembers somebody grabbing his shoulders, two reports like nearby gunfire, and then the pain. People to this day ask if he remembers the pain. Yeah, he remembers the pain—at least until the merciful moment when he became completely numb from the knee down.

Theismann recently said, "I can still close my eyes today and picture trainer Bubba Tyler on my left and Joe Gibbs on my right. It was at that point I also found out what a magnificent machine the human body is. Almost immediately, from the knee down, all the feeling was gone in my right leg. The endorphins had kicked in, and I was not in pain. I remember looking up and seeing Bubba being on my left side. I looked at him and said, 'Please call my mom and tell her I'm okay.' Joe was kneeling on my right side. He's looking at me, and he says, 'You mean so much to this club, and now you've left me in one heck of a mess.'"

The Redskins' orthopedic surgeon, Dr. Charles Jackson, was on the field in seconds. The doctor later recalled, "I was on the sidelines with my back to the play trying to reduce someone's jammed finger. I just remember L.T. coming over and grabbing me. I hadn't seen the play, and when I went out on the field, I looked down at Joe's leg and his bone was sticking through his sock. I'd only been doing this for three weeks, and I'm saying to myself, 'Oh, man, what have I gotten myself into here?' My first concern was to make sure pieces of grass or dirt or fibers from Joe's sock didn't get into his wound."

The doctor put on a pressure cast that went up to Theismann's knee.

In order to keep his thoughts together while this was going on, Theismann stared at the clock. It was a Longines clock. The time was 10:10. He saw the doctor and asked him how bad it was.

"Pretty bad," Dr. Jackson replied.

Theismann asked if they were going to be able to put the leg back together again.

The doctor said, "It already is."

Monday Night Football repeatedly showed the replay of the injury in excruciating slow-motion. Much of America was traumatized.

Theismann's stretcher was placed on a gurney, and he was slowly wheeled off the field. Among the players who came over to wish him the best was Giants veteran Harry Carson.

"Harry, I understand you're thinking of retiring," Joe said.

"Yeah, I am," Carson said, although he played for another three seasons after that.

"Well, don't go retiring, because I'm coming back," Theismann said.

"That may be the case," Carson said. "But it ain't gonna be tonight."

Theismann later recalled, "As they wheeled me out of that stadium, I got an ovation that I had never heard before in my life."

Theismann disappeared into the stadium, and the game resumed. Taking Theismann's place was backup quarterback Jay Schroeder, who had been drafted in the third round out of UCLA in 1984. He completed 13 of 20 passes during the remainder of the game for 221 yards, one touchdown, and no interceptions. L.T., as it turned out, may have knocked Theismann out of the game, but the Redskins only got fired up.

The injury forced Coach Gibbs to make a move that needed to be made anyway—the replacement of an aging quarterback with the new kid. The Redskins ended up winning the game 23–21, making it an ugly night in several ways for Giants fans everywhere.

"People break legs all the time in football. It involves the cracking of a bone, but most times, you can't see it," Dan Dierdorf later said. "That night, what you saw was so graphic, and when you watch something that's so far out of the normal, you just gag, but you almost can't help watching it again and again."

JOE IS FORCED TO WATCH

For 20 years Theismann refused to watch the videotape of his leg getting mangled.

"Why would I want to watch that?" was his standard reply when asked by a reporter. He had been around the TV when it was shown on a number of occasions but had always turned his head. He'd seen how others reacted to watching his injury, of course. No one laughed. People looked stricken. Nauseated. Why subject himself to that?

But in 2005 he agreed to watch the last play of his career while a camera recorded his reaction. The camera belonged to ABC, and the resulting footage was to be shown during an upcoming Monday night game.

After a couple of false starts—Theismann kept chickening out—he finally sat still for it. He still carries physical reminders of his injury. There's an ugly scar on his right shin about four inches up from his ankle. His right leg also healed an inch shorter than his left, and he wears a corrective shoe so he can walk without a limp.

"Let's do this," he said. "It's been long enough."

It was a media event, so there had to be suspense. They showed Theismann highlights of the first half and gave him a chance to talk about the groove he'd been in that night, how his performance was a major improvement over the mediocrity that had become the norm that year.

Theismann listened as the announcers that night—Frank Gifford, Joe Namath, and O.J. Simpson—called the game.

As the play approached, Theismann started to get antsy.

"This is funny," he said. "My heart's racing."

When the moment came, his initial reaction was almost disappointment. The live shot of the injury hadn't shown it in detail. He then watched the replay, taken by a camera on the other side of the field. "Oh," was all he said, and he jerked a little like everyone does at the snap of the bones.

"You could hear it," he said. "The pain was unbelievable. Oh, God. Wow. It just went so suddenly. It snapped like a breadstick. It sounded like two muzzled gunshots off my left shoulder—pow pow! How many times do I have to watch this?" He averted his eyes for the remaining replays.

Later he would say that the images were not as graphic as he had feared and that he was glad that they didn't have modern high-definition technology back then, or it would have been a hundred times more gruesome.

Ask anyone who saw that game how many replays ABC showed of the injury and they'll tell you hundreds, thousands. At least 20. The correct answer is three. ABC replayed Theismann's

BRYANT YOUNG: "A STEAMROLLER SNAPPING A FENCE POST"

Joe Theismann wasn't the only Giants opponent to sustain a gruesome leg injury during a televised game. It was Monday night, November 30, 1998, the 12th game of the season, and the Giants were playing the 49ers.

The warriors of Big Blue were getting their helmets handed to them. They were down 31–7 with a little more than seven minutes remaining in the fourth quarter. That was when San Francisco's Bryant Young's leg was turned into an accordion when his own teammate, Ken Norton, fell on him.

The injury was every bit as gruesome as Theismann's but not as famous. That was because ABC, perhaps having learned its lesson after making America cringe with repeated showings of the Theismann injury, only showed this one twice—once live and once on instant replay.

On the replay, the color commentator prefaced the footage by saying, somewhat urgently, "Turn away. Turn away if you don't want to see this."

In an article in the February 2000 issue of *Maxim*, Young described what happened. He said, "I was getting ready to put another sack on Kent Graham, the Giants quarterback. I even had my hand on his jersey. As usual there were lots of large bodies flying around."

He had just planted his right foot when Norton fell on the pile. The relationship between Norton and his leg, Young said, was like "a steamroller snapping a fence post."

On the field, the snapping of Young's bones sounded like gunfire, but Young didn't remember hearing any sound. "What I remember," he said, "is looking down and seeing my lower leg bent at an angle nature never intended: the shinbone's connected to...well, nothing." He said the image didn't upset him that much; he was too preoccupied with the pain.

gruesome injury only three times that night. It just felt like 300. The first time announcers did not warn the public, so most people didn't have a chance to look away.

After the first replay they cut to Theismann live, thrashing on the ground. There was clearly blood soaking though his sock. That was also disturbing, and they replayed the scene a second time almost immediately.

McCAFFREY BREAKS A LEG ON THE EVE OF 9/11

It was Monday night, September 10, 2001, when former Giant Ed McCaffrey, then a wide receiver for the Denver Broncos, broke his leg in the season opener versus the Giants. There were nine and a half minutes left in the third quarter. McCaffrey had just made a great catch for a 19-yard gain when he collided with Giants free safety Shaun Williams. He fell with his leg twisted up under him. The leg snapped below the knee, both the tibia and the fibula broken in two. McCaffrey was taken off the field and transported directly to the Swedish Medical Center in Denver.

The injury was pretty ugly, but it was immediately forgotten. The next day was 9/11, the day of the terrorist attacks on New York and Washington.

McCaffrey missed the remainder of the 2001 season but returned in 2002 and played for two more years before calling it a career.

That time Gifford issued a warning. He said, "If your stomach is weak, just don't watch." Later, in the third quarter, they showed the play for the third and final time, and again Gifford told squeamish viewers to avert their eyes.

The trouble was, the local news showed it a couple more times, and the Tuesday morning news shows showed it again until the very name "Theismann" made people shiver with horror.

WIDE RIGHT

At Super Bowl XXV, on January 27, 1991, the Giants once again won the ultimate game, but the way they got there—and how they won—couldn't have been more different than it had been four years before.

THE MAKEOVER AND THE SUB

To put it in modern terms, Bill Parcells liked to give veteran football players a makeover. He had great success trading for players thought to be past their prime and transforming them into players once again at their peak.

Parcells's most successful reclamation project was an aging running back named Ottis Anderson. Parcells made a deal that had diminishing returns written all over it and turned it into a home run. Under Parcells's tutelage, Anderson became a first-tier weapon.

Yes, they said Ottis Anderson was washed up. Then Anderson went out and became the MVP of Super Bowl XXV.

Anderson was a Florida kid who'd been a star at the University of Miami. He was drafted by the Cardinals and ran for 1,605 yards during his rookie year with St. Louis in 1979. Four more 1,000-yard seasons followed before Anderson's stats began to slip. In the NFL, diminishing returns tend to continue diminishing, and by the middle of 1986, the Cardinals were ready to get rid of him—and Bill Parcells saw something he liked.

In a move that raised an eyebrow or two, the Giants acquired Anderson midseason. Parcells needed a guy who could take time off the clock by getting him first downs on the ground, up the middle, and late in games.

The plan looked like a bust at first. Anderson was used sparingly during the remainder of 1986, and he was hurt in 1987. But by 1989 he'd worked himself into a starting role, and, improbably, he gained more than 1,000 yards for the 1989 Giants—a full five seasons after he'd last accomplished that feat. There is a rule of thumb that running backs start to slide quickly once they reach age 30. When Ottis Anderson got to the Super Bowl, he was 34.

Super Bowl XXV was played against the backdrop of the Gulf War. During the playoffs fans had grown accustomed to having games interrupted, although usually briefly, by the latest news bulletin out of the Persian Gulf—the latest missile attack, the latest military bombardment. These were particularly patriotic times, and the pregame fervor was jacked up a notch when Whitney Houston, in her prime, nailed the national anthem.

The Giants' starting quarterback that season had been Phil Simms. But in the third quarter of the Giants game against the Bills at Giants Stadium on December 15, Simms fell to the turf with an injured right foot. He was out for the year.

Simms was replaced with the Giants' longtime but seldom-used backup, 29-year-old Jeff Hostetler. Hostetler was in his fifth season with the Giants and had usually played well when Simms was injured—or if the Giants were ahead late and Parcells didn't want Simms getting hurt. It had been a frustrating experience for "Hoss," who felt in his heart of hearts like a starting quarterback. His multiple requests for a trade had all been ignored by the Giants.

Having a quality backup quarterback is a valued commodity for an organization, and as it turned out, the Giants' decision to hang on to Hostetler for all those years proved prescient. Some of Hoss's trade requests were borne out of frustration. The other major factor was boredom. He'd been a star at West Virginia and graduated in 1984. As a Mountaineer, Hoss passed for 321 yards in a big win at Oklahoma in his first game. He threw for 4,055 yards

Jeff Hostetler was Phil Simms's longtime backup. He was at the end of his fifth year with the Giants but had played only sparingly when he earned his second Super Bowl ring, this time as a starter.

in two seasons there after transferring from Penn State, where he'd been forced to play backup behind Todd Blackledge. Now he was a backup again. When Sundays came and he dressed and all he did was hold for place kicks—well, it drove him nuts. He volunteered to play on special teams just so he could see some action.

Going into Super Bowl XXV, Hostetler had started six NFL games—and won them all. In total, including all of his appearances, he'd thrown only 199 passes as a pro. Now they were printing up T-shirts by the thousands with his face on them.

Was he nervous?

"You prepare yourself," Hostetler said, "and you hope you could get into this situation, but actually, my past experience is that I've never really believed it until now."

Was he ready to become a starter when Simms went down?

"That's one of the things over the years," he said, "you learn not to be complacent, not to say, 'Well, I'm not going to play, so why study?'" He told reporters that there comes a time in many quarterbacks' pro careers when they admit to themselves that they aren't good enough to be starters, but he had never been able to do that. He believed he was good enough to start, and his performances on the field supported that fact.

Hostetler's frustration had peaked earlier that season. Simms had been playing great. The Giants were undefeated for a while. Before the season, Parcells said Hostetler might see some early action, but Simms had been playing so well that there was no need for a switch.

Hostetler did make one midseason appearance on October 21 in a game against the Phoenix Cardinals. Simms hurt his ankle in the first quarter, and Hostetler came in and led the Giants to a 20–19 victory. Remember that score.

Over the last few games Parcells had adjusted and tinkered with the Giants' offense so it would be less of a Phil Simms offense and more of a Jeff Hostetler offense.

"Fortunately," Parcells said, "we've had over a month to—I don't want to use the word *experiment*—but basically that's really what we were doing. We were just trying to pick and choose and let him execute some things in the game, and then talking to him about it and what he felt comfortable with."

Parcells's advice to Hostetler?

"Play the game," Parcells said. "Don't worry about making mistakes. You're not playing for the coaches, you're playing for the team. Just go play, and play within the structure, and we'll help you as much as we can. And don't worry about it."

To that point, Hostetler's stats on the season and postseason were pretty good. He'd completed 72 of 131 passes for 902 yards and one interception. He'd also run 48 times for 244 yards.

The Buffalo Bills were asked what they knew about Hostetler. Defensive end Bruce Smith said he remembered playing against Hostetler in college and knew him to be a tough SOB.

"I got a hit on him that I couldn't believe," said Smith. "Full speed, right in the chest. I didn't think he'd get up. He lay there for a few minutes, got up, staggered, and fell down again. Finally he got up, and they helped him to the sidelines. Three plays later, he came back in and threw a touchdown pass."

TREK TO TAMPA

To get to the Super Bowl, the Giants defeated the 49ers 15–13 in the NFC Championship Game. They managed to win that game, played January 20, 1991, at Candlestick Park in San Francisco, without scoring a touchdown.

Matt Bahr, in his 12th year in the league, hit field goals from 28, 42, 46, 38, and 42 yards. That accounted for all of the Giants' scoring. The difference in the contest was the Giants' ground game, which again and again marched the offense to within field-goal range.

The 49ers' running attack was not nearly as successful. The Giants rushed for 152 yards on the day, compared to the 49ers' 39 yards on the ground. Despite the ground domination, the 49ers still had the lead as late as the third quarter when they scored the game's only touchdown, a 61-yard scoring pass from Joe Montana to John Taylor, to make the score 13–6.

Bills kicker Scott Norwood pushes his potential game-winning field goal wide right, giving the Giants a 20–19 victory in Super Bowl XXV.

The winning field goal came late in the fourth quarter. Defensive tackle Eric Howard forced a fumble that was recovered by Lawrence Taylor in the last minutes. That led to the game-winning drive. The Giants were Super Bowl–bound for the second time in five years.

The site of Super Bowl XXV was Tampa Stadium in Tampa, Florida. Fans were told to arrive early because there were bound to be delays getting everyone into the stadium. Although we take stringent security measures at major sporting events for granted today because they have become the norm during the years following 9/11, back then pat-downs, bag searches, and metal detectors at the ballpark were a new and slightly frightening phenomenon. But with the war in the Persian Gulf raging, security couldn't be tight enough. Fans were issued little American flags before the game, and they waved them enthusiastically throughout the proceedings. On the big screen TV before the kickoff the fans were shown a film of our soldiers in the gulf. Fans were reminded that, in addition to the fans watching the soldiers, the soldiers were watching them. The troops in the Persian Gulf were getting the game on radio and satellite TV. Then George and Barbara Bush came on the TV, and the president spoke about how brave the soldiers were and how much they deserved our full support. Meanwhile, down on the field three huge floats were inflated, one of Mickey Mouse, one of Minnie Mouse, and the third of Goofy.

Finally, it was time for football.

The Giants and Bills traded field goals in the first quarter, Bahr striking first from 28 yards halfway through the first quarter. The Bills' place-kicker Scott Norwood evened things up on the subsequent drive, hitting from 23 yards away.

The teams had strongly contrasting styles on offense. The Bills used a no-huddle hurry-up, much more common today than it was then, and the Giants used up every second on the play clock in a constant effort to keep the clock moving. For that reason, the time-of-possession stat for the game, which shows the Giants having the ball for more than 40 of the game's 60 minutes, is misleading. The Bills only had the ball for eight minutes in the entire second half—thanks to the steady and eventually devastating production of Ottis Anderson.

The first touchdown of the game was scored by Don Smith of the Bills on a one-yard run early in the second quarter.

The Bills then pushed their lead to nine when Bruce Smith sacked Hostetler in the Giants' end zone for a safety.

The Giants finished the first half with their best drive of the game, which culminated in a 14-yard touchdown pass from Hostetler to Stephen Baker. Baker's touchdown reception came on a third-down play just before the half. The Giants made a decision to call a timeout to get that play in. Baker froze the defensive back to the inside in man-to-man coverage and showed great footwork after the catch.

The Giants' defense got a stop, and the ensuing offensive possession, their first of the second half, was methodical yet unstoppable, grinding, grinding, grinding, then ending with a one-yard Anderson touchdown run. Anderson scored on the 14th play of the drive, which burned a Super Bowl–record 9:29 off the clock. The key play was Mark Ingram's 14-yard reception on third and 13 from the Bills' 32. The Giants had gotten themselves into the third-and-long situation because of a questionable holding call. Ingram made two open-field, stop-and-start moves that nearly faked the tackler out of his shoes.

The Giants had fallen behind, but they came all the way back. Two other times during that incredible drive Hostetler had converted third downs through the air—an 11-yard pass to running back David Meggett on third-and-8, and a nine-yard pass to Howard Cross on third-and-4.

The Bills struck back on the first play of the fourth quarter when Thurman Thomas broke free and scored from 31 yards out, running over Myron Guyton on his way to the end zone. Cincinnati Bengals head coach Sam Wyche, a spectator at the game, later said, "It was just a great run on his part. There was a chance that the play could have been called back because there was a clip on the play. I'm not sure he could have made the tackle even if he hadn't been blocked from behind."

What turned out to be the final score of the game was a Bahr 21-yard field goal with 7:20 left in the game, giving the Giants a one-point lead. On that drive the Giants had a third-and-5 at the Bills' 9 and called time out. A pass to Meggett gave them a fresh set of downs. The Bills' defense buckled down at that point, and three plays later, the Giants settled for a field goal.

On their final drive, and with time left on the clock for one more play, the Bills sent out their field-goal kicking team. The attempt was from 48 yards. No gimme. Norwood's kick had plenty of distance but sailed wide right. The Giants were 20–19 victors and Super Bowl champions for the second time in five years.

SUPER BOWL XXV STARTING LINEUPS

Buffalo Bills Offense

Kent Hull, C
John Davis, G
Jim Ritcher, G
Howard Ballard, T
Will Wolford, T
Keith McKeller, TE
Al Edwards, WR
James Lofton, WR
Andre Reed, WR
Thurman Thomas, RB
Jim Kelly, QB

Buffalo Bills Defense

Jeff Wright, NT
Leon Seals, DE
Bruce Smith, DE
Cornelius Bennett, OLB
Darryl Talley, OLB
Ray Bentley, ILB
Shane Conlan, ILB
Kirby Jackson, CB
Nate Odomes, CB
Mark Kelso, FS
Leonard Smith, SS

New York Giants Offense

Bart Oates, C
Eric Moore, G
William Roberts, G
Jumbo Elliott, T
Doug Riesenberg, T
Mark Bavaro, TE
Steven Baker, WR
Mark Ingram, WR
Maurice Carthon, FB
Ottis Anderson, RB
Jeff Hostetler, QB

New York Giants Defense

Erik Howard, NT
Leonard Marshall, DE
Carl Banks, OLB
Lawrence Taylor, OLB
Pepper Johnson, ILB
Mark Collins, CB
Reyna Thompson, CB
Everson Walls, CB
Perry Williams, CB
Myron Guyton, FS
Greg Jackson, SS

While the Giants were still pouring champagne on each other, they'd already started to tease Hostetler.

"Hey Hostetler, you're just a backup," said Meggett.

"You can't win," added Mark Collins.

"Hey Hoss, John Madden said you can't do it. No backup quarterback has ever won a Super Bowl," Maurice Carthon threw in.

"How do you feel?" a reporter asked Hoss.

"I have a splitting headache, but I feel just fine," Hostetler replied.

Hostetler came by his headache honestly. He had been hammered a handful of times during the game. Luckily, all of the big hits had come on unsuccessful third-down plays, and Hostetler only had to make it as far as the sideline, where he had a few minutes to recover.

"I don't remember some of those hits," Hostetler said after the game. "Once or twice, if I had to go to the next play, I never would have made it."

Did he think he could win going in?

"I felt more confidence than any game I've ever played in," he said. "I felt confident with what I was trying to do. I was really excited to be in a Super Bowl, playing. I didn't have any nerves. I felt good. I just felt good."

Hostetler was reminded of a play he had made in the second quarter that might have turned the game around. On second down and 10 from the New York 7-yard line, the quarterback tripped over Anderson's right foot. He held the ball on his right hip and stumbled toward the goal line.

"I was dropping straight back, and I guess Ottis came inside because he saw Bruce Smith free on the inside real quick," Hostetler said. "So he tried to step inside, and I tripped over his foot, I guess. I was trying to regain my balance, and all of a sudden I felt this big paw trying to strip the ball. It was all over by then."

Even with Smith hungrily grabbing at his wrist, Hostetler didn't fumble. If he had, the Bills would have recovered the ball in the Giants' end zone for a touchdown, and the Bills would have been ahead 17–3, a deficit the Giants might not have been able to overcome. Giving up a safety is a lot better than giving up a touchdown.

Anderson was named the Super Bowl XXV MVP. Parcells wanted to execute a ground-control game, and Anderson took care of that. He had controlled the game, carrying the ball 21 times for a total of 102 yards. His longest run was 24 yards, and he scored a touchdown. He had lengthened drives with key first downs and kept the clock moving when the Giants had the ball.

If Norwood's kick had flown a few feet farther left, the MVP would have been Thurman Thomas, who gained 135 yards on only 15 carries, his longest run being his 31-yard touchdown scamper.

The stats for the game were just as close as the score. The Giants' offense gained a total of 386 yards. The Bills gained 371. The Giants gained 172 yards rushing, and the Bills gained 166. A big difference came in first downs, with the Giants leading 24 to the Bills' 18. (And, as mentioned, time of possession.) The Giants were also much better at converting third downs, going nine-for-16. The Bills only converted one third down in eight chances.

Both quarterbacks had good games, although not spectacular. There were no interceptions. Hostetler completed 20 of 32 passes for 222 yards and one touchdown. Kelly completed 18 of 30 for 212 yards.

Hostetler's favorite targets were Ingram and Bavaro, who had five catches apiece. Cross had four catches. The remaining six completions were spread out over four receivers: Baker, Meggett, Anderson, and Carthon.

In the locker room after the game Dave Anderson of *The New York Times* asked Bavaro which Super Bowl victory he enjoyed more.

"This one. Definitely this one," Bavaro said. That was a lot of talking for the usually tight-lipped tight end.

"How come?" the reporter asked.

SUPER BOWL XXV, JANUARY 27, 1991

New York 20, Buffalo 19

	1	2	3	4	Total
Bills	3	9	0	7	19
Giants	3	7	7	3	20

Attendance: 73,813

"I never thought I'd make it back here," Bavaro said, talking about Super Bowls and his knees and everything.

"Power wins football games. The idea was to play *power* football," Parcells, still wet from his Gatorade bath, explained to the gathered scribes. "We tried to wear them down. We almost didn't wear them down enough. Everybody assumed if we were down by one touchdown, we'd be out of it. But playing power football doesn't preclude you doing something else. We like to start with a power base."

About the defense, he said, "There were things they did during the year we were able to take away. Kelly held the ball more than he ever did." It was true. It seemed like Kelly was dropping back to pass all day and finding no one open, and no one getting open.

In the other locker room, Bills coach Marv Levy applauded Parcells's game plan. He said, "A team with a strong running game that can maintain ball control is not easy to beat at all. When you have the no-huddle, you don't have a lot of possession time. And when you don't score, you get rid of it fast. Every offense has its advantages and disadvantages, and maybe one of the disadvantages of that approach manifested itself today because of the offense the Giants have."

"The Bills went through the playoffs and ran roughshod over their opponents, and they haven't been in a close game," said Giants center Bart Oates after the game. "We're used to close games, like the game with San Francisco. We were in close games all along, and I think we were able to overcome that initial point of excitement and just do the things we had to do to win the game."

When the Giants' players and staff arrived back at Giants Stadium at 6:00 PM the next day, approximately 900 fans and four television crews were there to greet them. Parcells sat right behind the driver in the first bus. He looked out the window and marveled at the reception. The Super Bowl trophy was back in the second bus. Trainer Ronnie Barnes held the trophy up against the window so the fans could see it. There was pandemonium.

The New Jersey Sports and Exposition Authority had gone to the trouble of making a huge sign reading, "Welcome home,

Giants" and hanging it on the west end of Giants Stadium, but they hadn't counted on the Giants arriving back at the Meadowlands after dark, so the team couldn't see the sign. The fans had been there for hours. They'd been told that the Giants would be arriving at about 2:00, but the buses were four hours late. The crowd was loud but remained patient and orderly. The fans lined up so that the buses, escorted by a pair of state police cars, could drive by slowly so that everyone could get a glimpse of the silver trophy.

New Jersey Governor James Florio invited the team to a statehouse ceremony, but Wellington Mara said he was undecided on a celebration.

Elsewhere, New York Mayor David N. Dinkins issued a proclamation honoring the Giants and said he would present the keys to the city to Parcells and Giants management.

Despite the victory, there wasn't a lot of talk about doing it again the next year. There was no talk at all about this being the beginning of a dynasty. The team was savoring the moment, and everyone seemed to realize that this was going to be the last Super Bowl for the foreseeable future. When and if they ever returned to the NFL championship game, it was going to be with a different cast of characters.

They were a bunch of aging veterans battling injuries and battling time. Anderson was 34 years old. Phil Simms, inactive because of injury, was 35. Hostetler and Marshall were 30. L.T. and Oates were 32. Bavaro was only 27, but his knees were much older than that. Oates even had better offers. He'd passed the bar exam and graduated magna cum laude from Seton Hall Law School and was ready to start his new career at the law firm of his choice. Oates eventually went to five Pro Bowls (1990, 1991, 1993, 1994, 1995) before switching to real-estate law.

As he had done following Super Bowl XXI, Parcells gave interview after interview, always remembering to thank general manager George Young and co-owners Tim and Wellington Mara for supplying him with the players he wanted.

In the aftermath of the Super Bowl, Anderson faced an uncertain future. He had just completed his 12th season as an NFL running back—that was a very long career. His body had been battered and bruised for a long time. In one week he would become a free agent, and there was no guarantee that any team would want him. He wasn't even sure if he wanted to play anymore.

Asked about his status, Anderson said, "I want to finish my career as a Giant. I get tired of moving around. At my age, you don't want to keep moving. But if I get any offers…"

While he waited, Anderson packed his bags and went on a trip to entertain U.S. troops stationed in Saudi Arabia.

As it turned out, Anderson was brought back by the Giants, and he remained a Giant for two more years.

Parcells explained his decision to re-sign the aging running back. He said, "The track record doesn't mean anything. The MVP in the Super Bowl doesn't mean anything. I go by what I see. That's why O.J. Anderson is still with us. When you take him to training camp, and he doesn't miss any practices, and he's the best back you have, you've got to be nuts not to keep him."

Despite Parcells's optimistic words, Anderson's glory days were truly behind him. Although he appeared in 23 more NFL games after becoming Super Bowl MVP, he was to carry the ball only 63 more times for a total of 172 yards. After the Super Bowl, he would score only one more touchdown.

THE RUBBER SOLE DEPARTMENT

Not once, but twice the New York Football Giants have won the NFL championship while wearing sneakers, proving that sometimes necessity truly is the mother of invention.

THE 1934 SNEAKERS GAME

The New York Football Giants were born in 1925 when Tim Mara paid $500 for a franchise in the brand new National Football League. The college game was popular on Saturdays. Maybe, the new owners figured, there was a buck to be made on Sunday.

The Giants needed the "football" in their name to distinguish them from the baseball Giants. And distinguishing the two teams was necessary because both played in the horseshoe-shaped ballpark on East 155th Street in Manhattan. It was called the Polo Grounds, although no one ever played polo there. It nestled inside a geographical hollow known as Coogan's Bluff.

The pro football team didn't draw well in its first year and might have gone belly-up if it hadn't been for Red Grange, the famous college star, who came to town playing for the Chicago Bears. Grange's appearance drew more than 70,000 people to the Polo Grounds and kept the Giants franchise afloat. It was the largest crowd ever to see a pro football game. SRO tickets were sold by the thousand, and spectators were crammed anywhere there was room—in the aisles, on the ramps, on the field itself crammed right up to the sidelines. The gate receipts totaled $120,000, and Grange personally took home about a quarter of that.

What did Grange do to earn his $30,000? His stats aren't stunning, but they do demonstrate versatility. He carried the ball 13 times for 53 yards, returned two punts for 13 yards, caught a pass for 23 yards, and threw two completions for 32 yards. The "Galloping Ghost" justified his fee in many observers' opinions in the fourth quarter, when he intercepted a pass and ran it back 35 yards for the touchdown.

It wasn't a great day for the Giants, but it was a great day for pro football, which was still very much experimental and could have gone away forever if the sport's biggest star hadn't come to the sport's largest market. The Bears won the game 19–7, but the crowd went home happy. True-blue Giants fans were few—this was the first year of the team's existence, after all—and were greatly outnumbered by Grange fans. The biggest cheer of the game came when Grange ran back his interception for a touchdown.

Grange was such a strong draw that the following year he asked the NFL if he could start his own football team, which would play in Yankee Stadium, just across the Harlem River from the Polo Grounds. The Giants objected, and Grange instead started his own league, the old American Football League.

The Giants won their first NFL championship in 1927, with Earl Potteiger as their coach. In those days there was no championship game—you played out the season and the team with the best record was champ.

The Giants won that championship with the most dominant defense in team history. They allowed only 20 points for the season and finished 11–1–1. That's fewer than two points per game. It was not a league of parity. The stars of the defense were Steve Owen and Cal Hubbard. Hubbard later became the only player to be enshrined in both the Football Hall of Fame in Canton and the Baseball Hall of Fame in Cooperstown. Owen later became the Giants' coach.

In those early years there was no postseason. If two teams had the same record, the result of the regular-season game between the two determined the champion. That happened in 1929, when the Giants and Packers finished atop the league with 13–1–1 records. But the Packers beat the Giants during the season and so were declared the champions.

That year the Giants acquired the league's best player, Benny Friedman, who became the first to pass for more than 1,000 yards in a season. And despite the fact that the stock market crashed that December, the Giants enjoyed a growing popularity—averaging, for the first time, more than 25,000 people per game in home attendance.

In 1931 longtime Giants star Steve Owen was named head coach. He held the job for the next 23 years—and never had a written contract. An annual handshake between Owen and Mara was all that was needed.

During the 1930s the NFL began to see the value of postseason play. A single game to determine the big winner would draw well. So the teams were split into two divisions, with the two division winners meeting after the season for the championship.

The Giants first appeared in the NFL championship game in 1933. It was a fierce but disappointing battle against the Bears.

THE 1933 CHAMPIONSHIP GAME

The second championship game was held December 17, 1933, at Wrigley Field and was the first in which the Giants played. The game was played in a pea-soup fog, and the Giants led at the half, 7–6. Their touchdown came on a 29-yard pass from quarterback Harry Newman to Morris "Red" Badgro. The Giants also scored on a broken play that turned into a flea flicker, with Newman hitting Ken Strong for the eight-yard touchdown. But the Giants were done in on two plays initiated by Bronko Nagurski of the Bears. Nagurski threw an eight-yard touchdown pass to end Bill Karr. Nagurski later threw a jump pass, in which he jumped high in the air in order to see and throw the ball over a charging defender, to end Bill Hewitt, who then lateraled to Karr, who scored his second touchdown and won the game for the Bears.

The game was played before 26,000 fans in Wrigley Field on a day so foggy that it was hard for fans to see the game. After six lead changes, the Bears won 23–21.

The first truly legendary Giants game occurred the following year, on December 9, 1934. On that day, the New York Football Giants won the 1934 NFL championship game, a game that will forever be known as the "Sneakers Game."

Both the weather and the style of play were brutal. It wasn't as cold as the "Ice Bowl" game 33 years later, but there were sheets of sleet falling. The freezing rain had started the night before. By game time, the Polo Grounds looked more ready for ice hockey than for football.

The Giants were a heavy underdog in the game. The Giants were 8–5 on the season; the Bears, on the other hand, had won 13 games in a row and were unbeaten in their last 33 games. They were also the two-time defending champions.

The 1934 championship game was the third ever held. The first came in 1932, when the Bears defeated Portsmouth 9–0 to determine the league champion. That game had not been originally scheduled but was held because the Bears and the Spartans had both finished the regular season with 6–1 records.

As game time approached, sleet continued to fall, and the wind was whipping. Despite the horrid conditions, a crowd of greater than 35,000 had gathered at the Polo Grounds, which had been gussied up in honor of the importance of the game.

1934 NFL CHAMPIONSHIP GAME

Polo Grounds, December 9, 1934

	1	2	3	4	Total
Bears	0	10	3	0	13
Giants	3	0	0	27	30

Attendance: 35,059

Red, white, and blue bunting had been draped in front of the boxes.

The first half looked as if it were played in slow motion. Players who tried to run at full speed slipped and fell. Cleats provided no traction. The ice was too hard for football cleats to dig in.

For the Giants, however, help was on the way. Just before the game was to begin, with his team warming up on the field—as much as it's possible to warm up when it's arctic outside—Giants coach Steve Owen had an idea. He could see that both teams were slipping and sliding all over the place. Any player who tried to run at full speed inevitably ended up flat on his face.

The problem wasn't the ice, Owen realized—it was the football shoes. He told equipment manager Abe Cohen to run out and get some appropriate footwear for the team. Because it was a Sunday and many places were closed, Cohen had to go all the way to Manhattan College in the Bronx to get what he needed. There he picked enough pairs of sneakers—known as rubber-soled footwear at the time—to shoe the entire team.

At the end of the first half the Bears led the Giants 10–3. In the third quarter the situation only got worse. The Bears added a field goal and took a 10-point lead.

Then, late in the third quarter, the equipment manager finally arrived with the sneakers, and the Giants hurriedly changed shoes.

The fourth quarter began with the Giants running on rubber soles. And running and running. They scored on their first post-sneaker possession when rookie halfback Ed Danowski threw a 28-yard touchdown pass to Ike Frankian.

On the ensuing possession, the Giants' defense stopped the Bears, and, on the first play of the Giants' next drive, fullback Strong burst through a huge hole in the middle and ran for a 42-yard touchdown. The Giants had taken the lead for good.

Strong scored another touchdown on an 11-yard run, and Danowski finished with a running touchdown to go with his passing score, a nine-yard gallop around the right end. The Giants had scored four touchdowns in the final quarter for 27 points— they missed an extra point—to win the NFL championship. During the fourth quarter many fans jumped out of the stands

THE SUNNY SIDE OF THE FIELD

When the Giants played their first home game ever, in the Polo Grounds in upper Manhattan, Wellington Mara was nine years old. His dad owned the club, and the young Mara watched from the Giants side of the field, which happened to be the shady side.

When young Wellington caught a cold after the game—which the Giants lost 14–0 to the Frankford Yellow Jackets—his mother insisted that the Giants, from then on, take the sunny side of the field. That's the way it has been ever since, for the Giants' remaining years at the Polo Grounds, Yankee Stadium, the Yale Bowl, Shea Stadium, and Giants Stadium.

During the mid-1970s the Giants' coach, Bill Arnsparger, complained to Wellington Mara that it was a disadvantage to have the team on the sunny side. Not only did it mean looking into the sun, but it meant being on the opposite side of the field from the press boxes. Arnsparger felt vulnerable to espionage. The other team's assistant coaches, with binoculars, could watch and perhaps decode the Giants' signals. Arnsparger went to Mara and asked if the Giants could switch sides.

Remembering the time when he was nine and came down with the sniffles, Mara said, "Get better signals," and the Giants have remained in the sunshine to this day.

The Polo Grounds had a shady side and a sunny side, but no matter what stadium they call home, the Mara-owned Giants will always have their bench on the sunny side.

and onto the field, lining up along the sidelines and behind the end zones to get a closer look at the game. Several times the police had to halt proceedings to push surging fans off of the playing field. When the gun went off to signify the end of the game, fans rushed onto the west end of the field, and in less than two minutes, the goal posts were torn down.

After the game Bears back Nagurski said, "I think the sneakers gave the Giants an edge in that last half. They were able to cut back when running with the ball, and we couldn't cut with them."

On the Monday after the game a banquet was held at the Hotel Victoria, and NFL president Joe Carr presented the Ed Thorp Memorial Trophy, signifying the league championship, to the Giants.

Interestingly, the Giants had played the same 11 for most of the first half, making their first substitution with only minutes left before the half. Mel Hein, Butch Gibson, Tom Jones, Bo Molenda, Dale Burnett, Ike Frankian, and team captain Ray Flaherty played all 60 minutes.

Despite the fact that the NFL season was over and the Giants were the champions, the Giants still had three out-of-league games to play, against Paterson, New Jersey; San Francisco; and Los Angeles.

Walter Fleisher of *The New York Times* did some research into the history of rubber-soled shoes on the gridiron and found that Giants team captain Ray Flaherty had once worn sneakers in an icy college game. Flaherty played for Gonzaga University, and their sneakers game was against the University of Montana. Fleisher also learned that in 1933, the University of Washington football team wore sneakers on a frozen field for a game against the Seattle All-Stars and led 69–0 at halftime. The advantage was so great that Washington offered its opponents basketball shoes to wear for the second half, and the All-Stars took them up on their offer. The two teams played a scoreless second half. Giants player Bill Morgan, who had been a college star at Oregon, had attended that game and was the source of the information.

The Giants returned to the NFL championship game the next year.

SNEAKERS GAME II

Now some of you are scratching your heads and saying, "Hey, I heard of the Sneakers Game. I always thought it happened in the 1950s."

It did. That is, there was a second sneakers game. It was no coincidence that both games involved the Giants. When the weather was wet and cold during the days leading up to the 1956 NFL championship game versus the Chicago Bears at Yankee Stadium, Mara recalled the 1934 game and spoke to coach Jim Lee Howell about it.

Howell decided to conduct an experiment. He picked two normally sure-footed guys, defensive back Ed Hughes and back Gene Filipski. Hughes was told to put on his normal football shoes. Filipski was given a pair of basketball shoes to wear. Howell then had the pair go out on the Yankee Stadium skating rink and run routes. Filipski made his cuts with no problem, while Hughes went down a couple of times when he tried to change direction.

Seeing this, Howell went to defensive end Andy Robustelli, who moonlighted as the owner of a sporting goods store. Robustelli ordered 48 pairs of basketball shoes: black, high-rise, with rubber soles, sizes nine through 13.

The Giants and the Bears had played earlier in the season and had fought to a 17–17 tie. Anticipating another good show, the 56,836 in attendance cheered wildly right from the game's opening kickoff, which Filipski ran back 53 yards. The Giants quickly drove down the field and scored on a 17-yard touchdown run by Mel Triplett.

The Bears fumbled on their first possession, and the Giants capitalized with a field goal by Ben Agajanian, the man they called "Automatic." A three-yard touchdown run by Alex "Big Red" Webster followed, and the rout was on.

The only Bears score came on a turnover, when a botched punt set Chicago up on the Giants' 25-yard line, and from there they successfully drove in for the score.

It was 34–7 by halftime, and the Giants added 13 unanswered points in the second half. Much of the crowd, failing to see a

The Giants wore sneakers again for the 1956 NFL championship game and were again victorious, making them 2–0 in the rubber-sole department. Frank Gifford (left) and Charley Conerly celebrated the win in the Yankee Stadium locker room.

SNEAKER GAME II

NFL Championship Game, December 30, 1956

	1	2	3	4	Total
Bears	0	7	0	0	7
Giants	13	21	6	7	47

Attendance: 56,836

contest, left early and left happy. After all, it was about 20 degrees at kickoff and grew steadily colder as the afternoon wore on.

By the time the Giants poster boys had their say—a touchdown pass from Charley Conerly to Kyle Rote, and then another to Frank Gifford—the Yankee Stadium stands were largely empty. So many people had left to beat the traffic that there was traffic.

It would be nice to say wearing sneakers had directly resulted in the win, but that contention is exclusive to the first Sneakers Game. While getting trounced by the Giants, the 1956 Bears wore sneakers, too.

The victory brought the Giants their first NFL championship since 1938. That was a long wait for the shivering faithful of the Bronx. It was the second time that year that Yankee Stadium had been home to a world championship. A couple of months prior, the New York Yankees had defeated the Brooklyn Dodgers in the World Series behind the perfect-game pitching of Don Larsen.

Because of the weather, only 6,000 tickets were sold at the gate. Another 6,000 went unsold. Despite that, the gross receipts—$517,385, including $205,000 for TV and radio rights—set an NFL postseason record. The Giants players each received $3,779.19 for the championship. The Bears each received $2,485.16 in defeat.

TWO KICKS WE'D LIKE TO FORGET

Here are two stories of guys who tried to put the foot in football and instead brought nausea and dishonor to a proud franchise.

A QUICK KICK TO MAKE YOU SICK

One year after the original Sneaker Game, the Giants were back in the 1935 league championship game looking to defend their title. This time their opponents were the Detroit Lions, and the game was played in Detroit. For the third time in three years the title game was played under horrendous weather conditions. There was a mixture of wind, rain, sleet, and snow. The field, on the campus of the University of Detroit, was not frozen solid like the Polo Grounds in New York had been the year before; it was more of a frosty bog. The wind was such that the Lions only completed two forward passes all day. Both of those completions came in their first drive of the game, which resulted in a quick seven-point lead. The Lions touchdown came when running back Ace Gutowsky hammered his way in from two yards out. The Lions expanded their lead later in the quarter when Dutch Clark whirled his way like a top through the Giants' defense for a 40-yard score. Several times in the second half the Giants looked ready to change the momentum, driving down the field. But each time they were stopped short of scoring.

1935 NFL CHAMPIONSHIP GAME

University of Detroit Field, Detroit, Michigan, December 15, 1935

	1	2	3	4	Total
Giants	0	7	0	0	7
Lions	13	0	0	13	26

Attendance: 15,000 (approximately)

The low point in the game for the Giants came in the fourth quarter, when Ed Danowski tried to quick kick—punt unexpectedly on third down—in the gloppy field. Danowski only managed to kick the ball into the back of one of his linemen, and the Lions recovered the ball at the Giants' 26. Six plays later, Lions running back Ernie Caddell ran in for a four-yard touchdown. Buddy Parker of the Lions rushed for another score in the last seconds of the game to put the icing on the cake. The final score was Detroit 26, Giants 7, but the only play anyone remembered was Danowski's quick kick, which traveled maybe three yards and came to symbolize the Giants' mud-caked loss.

THE WORST PUNT EVER

The 1985 playoffs got off to a fine start. The Giants beat the 49ers 17–3 in the wild-card game and moved on to play the Bears in the divisional round. To get to their Super Bowl victory that year, the Chicago Bears first had to go through the Giants. The game was played at Soldier Field, and the wind was a-whipping.

It was one of those games, much like the quick-kick game, where little went right for the Giants and everything went right for their opponents. Yet, still, there was a goat. There was one play that was so bad that it became the symbol of the futile effort, the one thing everyone remembered—Bears fans with giggling delight and Giants fans with an embarrassed groan and suddenly unsettled stomachs.

With the game still scoreless, the Bears had the Giants backed up deep into their own territory and facing a fourth down. Rookie punter Sean Landeta ran onto the field and took his position near his own goal line. The snap was good, but somehow, the wind caught the ball between Landeta's hands and his foot and he all but missed it.

As Gary Myers of the *New York Daily News* put it, "The ball grazed off his foot, sort of like a foul tip."

As Bears coach Mike Ditka wrote in his book *In Life, First You Kick Ass*:

> People who know about the Midwest and the Great Lakes may not have a clue about wind coming in off Lake Michigan or the wind swirling around in places like

New York Giants punter Sean Landeta actually whiffed on a punt deep in his own territory during a 1985 playoff game at windy Soldier Field in Chicago.

Cleveland or Buffalo off Lake Erie. In Chicago, Soldier Field is right next to the lake, and the cold wind will come in and do whatever it wants. Sometimes you'll see flags flying in all four directions.... Early in the game we back the Giants up toward their own goal at the north end, and it's fourth down. The wind is gusting, and it's something like 14-below-zero wind chill. The snap comes back for Sean Landeta, their punter, and we've got a punt-block rush on from the left side with Shaun Gayle and Dennis Gentry. They pick up the rushers, but Landeta is worried or hurried or something and he goes to punt the ball and swings his leg as hard as he can and misses it. He misses the freaking ball. Maybe he gets a tiny piece of it, but the wind just moves the ball to the side, and it looks like Charlie Brown trying to kick the ball after Lucy yanks it away.

When Landeta got to the sideline, he had the high beams of Bill Parcells focused on him.

"What happened?" the coach asked.

"I missed it," Landeta said.

"You what?" Parcells screamed.

Any chance the Giants might have had evaporated with that play. The final score was 21–0. The Giants rushed for a grand total of 32 yards that day—and it was too windy to pass.

You might think that Landeta, a native of Baltimore who went to Towson University, would have crawled under a rock after that game, never to come out and face the public again. But that didn't turn out to be the case. On the contrary, the 1985 season was just the first of eight and a half he'd play with the Giants. And after leaving Big Blue, Landeta punted for the Rams, Buccaneers, Packers, and Eagles before retiring in 2005.

ROUGH STUFF

There have been times in Giants history when the phrase "unnecessary roughness" didn't quite cover it. Here are just a couple of moments that got out of hand.

THE FOG GAME

On December 11, 1938, the Giants defeated the Green Bay Packers at the Polo Grounds 23–17 and won what would turn out to be their last NFL championship in quite a while. Just before the kickoff, Mel Hein received the Gruen Award, a watch signifying him as the Pro Football Player of the Year.

The 48,120 spectators who attended the game despite it being a dark and damp day broke the old NFL record for largest crowd to attend a championship game. It broke the old record by more than 13,000.

By the end of the game, which began at 2:00 PM, it got so dark—both from the dank weather and from the setting sun—that floodlights were turned on beside the field (the Polo Grounds didn't yet have lights on the roof). According to one writer, the lights served to illuminate some of the "rough stuff that was going on down there."

After the game, Louis Effrat of *The New York Times* reported the scene as the happy Giants celebrated in their Polo Grounds dressing room and Coach Owen went around and personally congratulated every Giant with a handshake and a hug.

Mel Hein was one of the heroes of the 1938 championship team.

"I'd particularly like to praise the great work of Hank Soar, Ed Danowski, Tuffy Leemans, Ward Cuff, Mel Hein, Ed Widseth, Jim Poole, Jim Lee Howell, and Orville Tuttle. I think we proved beyond a doubt that we were not lucky when we beat the Packers the last time. Our blocking was great," Owen said.

Hein was so joyous over the victory that he seemed oblivious to the large, egg-shaped bruise on his cheekbone, where he'd been kicked by a Packer. Back in the days before face masks, that stuff happened all the time.

70

Over in the other locker room, Green Bay Packers coach Curly Lambeau, after whom Lambeau Field in Green Bay is named, didn't have much to say after the game about the Giants' blocking, but he had plenty to say about two controversial calls by linesman Larry Conover.

"I don't want to say this in the form of an alibi, but in my opinion Conover was definitely wrong when, in the second period, he ruled Tuffy Leeman's pass to Len Barnum complete. Moving pictures of the play will prove that Barnum fumbled immediately, the ball going out of bounds, and that the receiver did not hold it long enough to establish possession. Since that play led to a Giants touchdown, Conover's decision hurt us plenty.

"Then," Coach Lambeau continued, "late in the last quarter, Arnold Herber threw a first-down pass to Milt Gantenbein, our end, and Conover called Gantenbein an ineligible receiver, although how he arrived at such a conclusion is beyond me because Bernie Scherer, our other end, was at least a yard behind the line of scrimmage. So instead of us being in possession in Giants territory, New York took over in our zone. The movies will prove that I'm right about this play, too."

Reporters asked if there would be a formal protest of the game, and Lambeau said no.

Coach Owen was asked for his version of the ineligible receiver play, and Owen said Lambeau had seen it all wrong. He said, "Why, Gantenbein and Scherer were playing side by side on the line at the time, and it's to Conover's credit that he called the play as he saw it. As for the other play, it's a matter of opinion, and mine is obvious."

Veteran official Tom Thorp, who wasn't involved in the controversy said the game itself was great, possible blown calls aside. "It was the best played and most exciting game I have ever worked on or seen," Thorp said.

On the morning after the game the Giants coaches and players met at 11:00 AM in the Whitehall Hotel for a victory breakfast. By winning the championship, the team had earned the right to play a Pro All-Star team in Los Angeles on January 15, 1939.

Coach Owen told the men at breakfast that they should enjoy their New Year's celebrations and return for practice on January 2.

Because the players received a percentage of the gate receipts, the large crowd netted each Giants player $504. The Packers got $369 each.

WALL STREET FISTICUFFS

Stories don't get much rougher than this one. Any time you can combine a grandfather, a choke hold, and the New York Stock Exchange, you know you have a tale for the ages.

According to a report in the *New York Post*, Stephen Mara, a third-generation Giants owner and son of the late Wellington Mara, was on the floor of the NYSE on the Tuesday following the Giants' 36–22 loss in 2006 to their hated rivals from Philadelphia.

A veteran floor trader by the name of Bob Tomasulo, a 57-year-old grandfather and Eagles fan, spotted Mara and decided that a little gloating was in order. Tomasulo and Mara had what Tomasulo called a "friendly sports rivalry" going back several years; before the game Mara reportedly boasted, "We're gonna kick your guys' you-know-what."

"Probably," Tomasulo is alleged to have replied.

Biting dialogue like that you couldn't make up.

Before we get to the real action, here's a little background: earlier in the season the Giants' defensive players had taken to miming a basketball jump shot after making a sack or otherwise impressive play. The practice had been discontinued when the Dallas Cowboys, badly beating the Giants one afternoon, began to imitate the jump-shot move in a mocking way. And so, when Tomasulo saw Mara on the floor of the stock exchange, he made the jump-shot move and said, according to reports, "Maybe you have a basketball team instead of a football team."

At that point, according to witnesses, Mara started screaming, "I'm gonna f*ckin' kill you! Don't f*ck around with my family! Don't insult my family!"

Tomasulo is said to have replied, "Hey, what is your problem? It's just a game!"

THE SAD LIFE OF BOBBY JOHNSON

Earlier in the book, when describing the Giants' push toward their first Super Bowl victory, we called the pass from Phil Simms to Bobby Johnson that converted a fourth-and-17 the most clutch play in franchise history.

We know how well Simms turned out, and we'd love to report that Johnson had that kind of luck as well. But that's not the case. That first Super Bowl season was Johnson's last with the Giants, and his luck just went south from there.

He was traded to the Chargers in August 1987, after he tested positive for marijuana and cocaine. The Chargers cut him three weeks later, and his pro football career was over. His cocaine addiction was so severe that he quickly spent all of his money.

He managed to get a job working in a pencil-making factory in his hometown of Shelbyville, Tennessee, but, in a hideous accident, got his hand caught in a pencil-making machine and lost three fingers on his right hand.

His fingers were not cut off, they were pulled off by the strong vacuum of the machine. He found his fingers on the far side of a roller, as "flat as popsicle sticks."

"I had to pull my arm back out because my body was going in, too," he said during a recent interview. According to the *New York Daily News*, Johnson had skin grafted from his stomach and thigh. There is a large chunk of skin in place of his fingers that looks like a slab of meat. "My hands, that was my pride," he said.

After that came years of sleeping on park benches, in missions, or, while he still had one, in his car. He tried many jobs, but nothing worked out. He's worked at a medical supply company, in a steel factory, at a DVD distribution center, and at a storm-door factory.

Today, we're pleased to report, he's off drugs, but he's still broke and is now living in his mother's small apartment.

"No, it's not just a game. It's my f*cking family!" Mara allegedly replied.

"Mara just snapped," Tomasulo later said. "He charged me like an animal. He charged me like he wanted to sack me. At first he got me into a bear hug and bent me over a trading post. At first I thought it was a joke. Then he proceeded to choke me. I passed out for a minute."

A witness said that immediately following the altercation Mara "walked back to his booth and was kind of laughing it off."

Mara commented, "This guy and I have gone back and forth for years about the Giants and the Eagles. He came to work with every intention of pushing my buttons. And he did. And I reacted. I reached out to him to apologize for my part in this unfortunate incident, but we have yet to speak."

A friend of Mara's who witnessed the scene told the *Post* that the altercation was blown out of proportion: "They exchanged words and there was a brief tussle, and it didn't amount to anything. Coworkers have ribbed Mara for years about the team, and after a while it has to get to somebody. Mara has for years handled himself with a certain grace and style responding to all this. A lot of these guys probably wished their families owned the Giants, and since they don't, when the team loses, they taunt him."

Tomasulo made it clear that his lawyers felt "this was a very serious incident. The doctors told me I have a bruised larynx. My blood pressure spiked to 260 over 140."

When asked why he hadn't taken the phone call from Mara during which Mara hoped to apologize, Tomasulo said, "I wasn't in the mood to talk to him. I'm 57 years old, and I've been bullied and pushed around a lot in my life. I grew up in Brooklyn. I'm kind of sick of taking it."

IN THE CLUTCH

Sometimes guys step up at key moments and do things they've never done before, often when the adrenaline is pumping hardest and the fear of failing is most excruciating.

"HE CAN'T KICK IT THAT FAR"

The 1958 Giants did not get off to a fast start. Despite a coaching staff that was jam-packed with future legends—future Packers head coach Vince Lombardi and future Cowboys head coach Tom Landry were both on Jim Lee Howell's staff that season—and a team with many veteran stars—such as Frank Gifford, Kyle Rote, Sam Huff, and Roosevelt Grier—the team lost their last five pre-season games and split the first four games on the schedule.

In the meantime, the Cleveland Browns, behind Jim Brown, perhaps the greatest running back ever, went undefeated during that same time span.

The Giants played hard and went on a winning streak. By the 12th and last game of the season, the Giants trailed the Browns by one game. The schedule-makers obviously knew what they were doing because the Giants were slated to play the Browns on the season's final Sunday.

In essence, to get to the championship game, the Giants would have to play and beat the Browns twice in a row because the first win would result in a tie, which would be followed by a

Sam Huff

one-game playoff. Back in those days, there was only overtime in playoff and championship games. Since this was neither, the game could conceivably end in a tie. If that were the case, the Browns would have won the division and the Giants' season would have been over.

Browns coach Paul Brown's offense was not difficult to figure out, it was just hard to stop. He had the best running back in the business, so he'd punch the ball up the middle using Jim Brown. When it came time to cross up the defense, the Browns would complete short passes in the flat, over the middle, always under rather than over the defensive secondary. Only when the defense had bunched at the line of scrimmage in an attempt to stop this short game would the Browns pass downfield.

The Giants' assistant coach, Tom Landry, believed that the Browns offense was more than just dull, more than just methodical. He believed it was predictable. This was a world in which there were no computers, but the Giants didn't need a computer: they had Landry. He made a complete study of which plays the Browns ran and when. He made lists and more lists of game situations, both by score and by down, and came up with a proper defense for each situation the Giants might encounter. He knew just how many running plays the Giants would have to stop before Brown would call for a passing play, and he knew the exact order in which the Browns would run their passing plays once that time came.

Andy Robustelli was a defensive end who played from 1951 to 1955 with the L.A. Rams before joining the Giants for another nine seasons. Robustelli recalled that Landry's defensive game plan was precise when it came to predicting what the Browns were going to do. Years later, Robustelli recalled the 1958 season and a Cleveland Browns team that could seemingly beat everyone—except the Giants.

"Landry used to tell us that people have habits and can only do certain things," Robustelli recalled. "If a player can only run outside, coaches program him to do just that. If you are facing a good passing quarterback, then you know you will see a lot of passes. 'Trump your aces,' he'd say. He'd always tell us we'd match our defenses against what the other guy does best and not worry about what he won't or can't do."

Against the Browns the Giants' defense positioned itself on the field in a 4-3 alignment. It was innovative at the time but widely imitated across the NFL in the years that followed. The Giants' defensive starters were Robustelli, Dick Modzelewski, Roosevelt "Rosey" Grier, and Jim Katcavage up front; Harland Svare, Huff, and Cliff Livingston behind them; and Carl Karilivacz, Lindon Crow, Jim Patton, and Emlen Tunnell playing back.

That defense could swarm into an intended hole when the opponents ran and often made the quarterback unload the ball before he wanted when they passed. Landry was confident that if

Charley Conerly
(Photo courtesy of
Bettmann/Corbis)

anyone could stop Jim Brown and company it was the Giants' defense.

Landry's confidence took quite a blow when, on the first play of the game, on a snowy December 14, 1958, the Browns' offensive line blasted a hole in the Giants' defense and Brown plowed through the defenders that remained, galloping 65 yards through the snow for a touchdown. The legendary Lou "the Toe" Groza (who, as late as the 1960s, kicked extra points with a cigarette in his hand) kicked the extra point and made the score a super-quick 7–0.

The Browns might have felt cocky and the Giants shaky at that moment, but little did they know that Brown's first-play touchdown was going to amount to almost half of the Browns' offense for the day. In the remainder of the game, they only managed 83 more yards of offense.

Pat Summerall kicked a 46-yard field goal, a long one for him, and Groza responded later in the second quarter with a 22-yarder of his own. The score was 10–3 Browns at the half.

The Giants back in those days ran a halfback option: quarterback Charley Conerly would pitch the ball out to halfback Frank Gifford, who would sweep right behind three linemen. He then had the option of running with the football—the option he chose the great percentage of the time—or throwing the ball upfield. During halftime, Giants flanker Kyle Rote noticed that the Browns defense had begun to assume that Gifford would run on that play. Rote, a potential pass receiver on the play, told Conerly he was losing his defenders each time they ran the option.

Gifford later recalled that they didn't use the play right away when the second half started. "We sat on it and waited for the right time," he said. As it turned out, the right time came with

Frank Gifford (left) and Alex Webster (Photo courtesy of Getty Images)

Kyle Rote
(Photo courtesy of
Bettmann/Corbis)

only five minutes left in the game, with the Browns still ahead by a touchdown.

Brown had slipped and fallen on the ice and coughed up the ball, causing a big change in momentum. The Giants had the ball on the Browns' 45. They ran the halfback option. Gifford took the ball to the right behind his three blockers. Rote faked a block and headed upfield. Gifford hit Rote with a pass, and Rote, not as fast as he'd once been, was tackled at the Cleveland 6. After two attempts to power the ball over the goal line with runs up the middle, the Giants ran a second halfback option, and again Gifford threw the ball, this time to tight end Bob Schnelker in the end zone. Summerall's extra point tied the score.

Remember, the Giants had to win the game—a tie would have given the Browns the conference title. So the Browns were in no hurry. This was before the days of play clocks and modern technology. It was much harder to get a delay-of-game penalty. After the ball was spotted, one of the officials would start counting one-Mississippi, two-Mississippi, so it was easy for slow-moving pro football players to kill almost a minute between plays. The Browns might have been better served to try to get a first down rather than to burn as much time as possible off the clock. They ran three running plays up the middle and lined up to punt. The Giants went all-out to block the kick, and the hurried punt went only to midfield. Conerly took the Giants to the Browns' 29 when the drive stalled, and Summerall was called upon to kick a 36-yard field goal.

Summerall had made a long field goal earlier in the game, but the weather was deteriorating. He later admitted that he was nervous. He'd been hot and cold all year, and things weren't helped by a knee injury he'd suffered the previous week.

The resulting field-goal attempt was right out of Summerall's worst nightmare. He poorly kicked the ball, which knuckled up into the wind, bent left, and fell short. Summerall was convinced that he was destined to be the goat of the game and the season.

He later admitted that he wanted to stay on the field and play defense so he'd have an opportunity to make up for his error. But he was called to the bench, where he sat with his head hung low while teammates patted his back and told him to forget it.

Summerall said, "Then [guard] Cliff Livingston came over and said, 'We'll get the ball back. You'll get another shot.' Then I truly believed I would."

The Giants' hopes were again helped by Browns punter Dick Deschaine, who shanked another one, giving New York the ball at midfield. The weather was worse than ever. Snow swirled over the field, creating almost white-out conditions. A blanket of snow covered the field. The yard markers were invisible.

On third and long, the Giants went for it all. Conerly put up a bomb that hit receiver Alex Webster right in the hands for what would have been a sure touchdown, but Webster dropped the ball.

Webster later told Summerall, "If I had caught that pass, no one would have ever heard of you."

It was fourth and long at the Browns' 42. The goal posts were on the goal line in those days, so when Summerall was sent onto the field to attempt a field goal longer than any other he'd ever kicked—even when he was younger and had two good knees and the weather was perfect—Yankee Stadium became eerily quiet.

If Summerall had any confidence at all, it was destroyed on the sideline when he heard offensive coach Vince Lombardi anxiously trying to talk head coach Jim Lee Howell out of attempting the field goal, singing the praises of a Hail Mary pass instead. Howell would have none of it and sent Summerall onto the field with the words, "Go kick it!"

Conerly was the holder and was busy preparing a spot for Summerall to kick from, brushing snow away and making sure there was nothing to prevent a good hold. The Browns' defense crowded the line of scrimmage, snarling and drooling. With the defensive line getting a little too eager, the Browns linebackers began to scream, "Stay on sides! Stay on sides!"

The official scorekeeper would later say that the ball was kicked from the 49, but there was no way of telling precisely. Some estimate that it was as much as four yards farther away than that.

Unlike his earlier miss, Summerall hit the ball squarely this time. The result was a true end-over-end kick.

"I knew the second I hit it that it was far enough," Summerall later recalled. He thought he started to see the ball float to one side, but by the time it got to the 10-yard line, it had straightened itself out and went just inside the right upright. The ball didn't come down until it had reached the back of the end zone.

Yankee Stadium exploded in joy. On the sideline Vince Lombardi—he of little faith—came over to Summerall and said, "You know you can't kick the ball that far, don't you?"

There was a little more than two minutes left in the game. The Giants' defense got the stop they needed, and the Giants' offense ran out the clock. Looking back on that famous kick, Summerall said, "I couldn't believe Jim Lee was asking me to do that. That was the longest attempt I'd ever made for the Giants. It was on a bad field, and it was so unrealistic. Most of the fellows on the bench couldn't believe it, either. No one knows how far it had to go. You couldn't see the yard markers. The snow had obliterated them. But it was more than 50 yards, I'll tell you that."

Up in the press box, Wellington Mara recalled thinking, "He can't kick it that far. What are we doing?"

After the game, Tim Mara, the old man, said, "What a kick. What a kicker. But what the hell? That's what I pay him for, and I'm glad to see he earned his money today."

The following week the Giants' defense, guided by Tom Landry's prognostications, held the Browns scoreless, and the Giants won 10–zip. Jim Brown was squelched. The Browns got frustrated early.

The Giants' Mel Triplett was ejected from the game in the second quarter for fighting. Afterward he pleaded his case, saying, "Paul Wiggin kicked me, and Don Colo grabbed the bar of my mask. That's when we started to go at it. It was just one of those things. But the officials ought to know that it takes two to make a fight."

The most memorable play of the game was sent in by offensive coach Vince Lombardi, who was known to his players at the time as Vinnie. The Giants had the ball on the Browns' 19. Conerly took the snap and handed off to Webster. A double reverse followed, in which the ball ended up in the hands of Frank Gifford, who waited until he was just about to be tackled and lateraled back to Conerly, who ran the ball in for a touchdown. The Giants later claimed that the entire play, including the last lateral to the 37-year-old Conerly, went off just as designed on the chalkboard, but the Browns refused to believe it.

"Coach," Brown said incredulously, "the double reverse didn't surprise me. But the lateral to Conerly? That couldn't have been planned."

From there, the Giants went to the NFL championship game, where they met the Baltimore Colts in what has been called the greatest game ever played.

PAT SUMMERALL

Pat Summerall grew up in Lake City, Florida, and was a tennis and bas-ketball star in high school. He won the Florida State Tennis Championship and twice won All-State basketball honors. It was at the University of Arkansas that he was first noticed for his gridiron skills. He graduated with honors from Arkansas in 1952, with a degree in educa-tion. (He later returned to school and earned his master's degree in Russian history.) Even after he became a kicker for the Giants, he contin-ued to play other sports during the off-season and spent a brief time playing baseball in the St. Louis Cardinals organization.

Most of you who remember Summerall don't remember him as a kicker, but as the longtime legendary sports announcer. Indeed, Summerall has been a TV announcer for more Super Bowls (16!) than anyone else. For 10 other Super Bowls he did the radio broadcast. Since the first Super Bowl in January 1967, he has been in attendance for all but one.

After he retired from football following the 1961 season, he was immediately signed by CBS Sports, and he became a signature voice for that organization for the next 32 years. In 1994 he and his broadcast partner, John Madden, moved to the Fox network and continued calling football games together. The Summerall and Madden announcing team was considered by many to be the strongest in NFL history and was together for 21 years before Summerall's retirement in 2002. Summerall and Madden hold the record for calling the most-watched sports program. Their call of Super Bowl XVI in 1982 was watched by almost half of all the TVs in the country.

He began his broadcasting career even before he retired from foot-ball. In 1960 he began doing spot jobs for CBS. He immediately proved that he wasn't just a football expert. He could comment on any sport and sound like a lifelong expert. In addition to football, he became the voice of CBS golf, tennis, basketball, and boxing. From 1960 until 1971 he was sports director of WCBS Radio in New York City.

His trophy shelf is full. He has received the Lifetime Achievement Award for Sports from the National Academy of Television Arts and Sciences, the Pro Football Hall of Fame's Pete Rozelle Radio-Television Award, the NFL Alumni's prestigious Order of the Leather Helmet, Sportscaster of the Year honors from the National Sportscasters and Sportswriters Association, the Lifetime Achievement Award from the National Quarterback Club, the Golden Mike Award from the Touchdown Club of America in 1977, the Association of Tennis Professionals' JAKS Award as Tennis Broadcaster of the Year in 1983, and an honorary doctorate degree. He received the George Halas Award in 2002, which had only been presented three times before, to Rozelle, Halas, and Art Rooney. Today Summerall lives in Southlake, Texas. He is founder of Summerall Sports Ltd., a contributing partner of Pat Summerall Productions, and host of cable television's *Champions of Industry* and *Summerall Success Stories*.

Pat Summerall

GIANTS VS. BROWNS

Yankee Stadium, December 14, 1958

	1	2	3	4	Total
Browns	7	3	0	0	10
Giants	0	3	0	10	13

Attendance: 63,192

LI'L BROTHER PULLS ONE OUT IN PHILLY

Fran Tarkenton's 1970 comeback is still the biggest in Giants history, but the Giants came close to matching it on September 17, 2006, against the Eagles. The game was played on Sunday afternoon at Lincoln Financial Field. The Giants were behind 24–7 in the fourth quarter, and Eli Manning—a struggling young quarterback in the shadow of a superstar older brother and badly in need of a confidence boost—led the Giants back to a 30–24 overtime victory. The heroes of the game were Manning, who passed for 371 yards; Amani Toomer, who caught 12 passes—two for touchdowns; and Plaxico Burress, who caught the game-winning score.

The Giants had cut the deficit to 24–14 early in the fourth quarter, when Burress caught a pass but had it knocked out of his hands by defender Brian Dawkins. Luckily, Giants wide receiver Tim Carter recovered the fumble and managed to score.

Carter later recalled, "I was on the other side of the field and I saw Plaxico make the catch, and I saw him try to break the tackle and he got hit and I saw the ball fly out. I saw a couple of guys go after the ball, and I thought it might get kicked around. I went after it—and I won. I was aware of where I was, and I knew I might be able to get into the end zone."

On the ensuing Eagles drive, Brian Westbrook fumbled, and safety Will Demps recovered at the Philadelphia 33. Four minutes were left. A Manning pass to Toomer with 3:28 left in the fourth quarter cut the Eagles' lead to 24–21.

Eli Manning has been hot and cold his first few years in New York, but he pulled out a historic overtime win on the road in Philadelphia on September 17, 2006.

The Giants got the ball back at their own 20-yard line with 58 seconds left and no timeouts. Manning drove the Giants down the field—boom, boom, boom—each receiver tiptoeing out of bounds and the Giants hurrying up to the new line of scrimmage.

They made it to the Eagles' 32 with seven seconds left when Eagles defensive end Trent Cole was called for an untimely personal foul. The Giants then tied the game with a Jay Feely 35-yard field goal.

There was a controversial play on what would turn out to be the winning drive. Manning threw to Visanthe Shiancoe, and the ball was caught simultaneously by the intended receiver and Eagles defender Dawkins. Eagles fans believed it was an interception, but the officials decided it was a catch for Shiancoe and a

Giants first down. (After the game Dawkins told the Associated Press, "From my vantage point, I had two hands on it and both feet down, and then it carried over to his one arm. Nothing you can do about it now.")

The overtime began with the teams trading punts. The Giants got the ball for the second time at their own 14. Tiki Barber was given the ball, and he cracked off 16 yards in two carries. Two passes to Toomer followed, for a total of 15 more yards. A few plays later Manning went to Toomer again for a first down at the Eagles' 30. Manning handed off to Brandon Jacobs for a nine-yard gain, then to Jacobs again for six more. The Giants were at the 15, but only briefly, as a holding penalty on Tim Carter pushed the ball back to the 25. A couple of unsuccessful plays followed. And so it was, with only 3:19 left in overtime, the Giants had the ball third-and-11 at the Eagles' 31. Manning, avoiding a blitz, saw Burress in the end zone and heaved one up in his direction. Burress was covered in the end zone by cornerback Sheldon Brown, but Burress's height and jumping ability helped him win the "jump ball" pass from Manning.

Manning gushed after the game, "It was a huge win. It wasn't the prettiest one. It was downright ugly for us for a while. We couldn't get anything going. At the end there I was tired. I was telling myself one more play. There's no place better to get a win than Philadelphia."

Manning didn't have to say why. It was because Eagles fans and players are, even by NFL standards, so nasty.

Burress, too, enjoyed doing it in Philly. He said, "There's no better place to get a win than to come into Philadelphia and beat them in their own stadium. Their players had a couple of things to say about us this week. They came out and got after it after we scored on our first drive and we kept plugging away. It's so gratifying to get a win *here*."

Coach Tom Coughlin, as usual, wasn't being nearly as cool as he probably wanted to be. He was gushing with joy just like everyone else. "That was fun," Coughlin said. "When we were down 24–7, not much was going well. But I just told the players that I saw a little glimpse of New York Giant pride there in that second half. They kept coming back, and they kept fighting back little by little. It wasn't pretty, but it was effective."

Michael Strahan emphasized the drama, saying, "We're on the road, we're down 17 going into the fourth quarter in Philadelphia, the fans are cursing at us, screaming at us, yelling obscenities at us, mooning us on the way in. To win in this hostile territory and have it end on such a good play—priceless."

The comeback came in the Giants' second game of the season, their first victory. In week one, the Giants had lost to the Indianapolis Colts and Eli's older brother Peyton on *Sunday Night Football*, and Eli had to spend the week answering questions about how it felt to be not quite as good as his big brother. It's safe to say that Eli entered the game feeling like he had something to prove, and, almost four hours later as he savored his victory, he felt his point well-made.

Eli Manning was sacked eight times during the game, but managed to pass for 371 yards, with three touchdowns. He completed 31 of 43 attempts with just one interception.

THE TITTLE YEARS

They called him the Bald Eagle, but he saved his best years for the Giants.

1961: A VERY GOOD YEAR

Following the 1960 season, a new era of Giants football began, and for some oldsters it was the most beloved of all. The winds of change began blowing when, after seven years as Giants head coach, Jim Lee Howell announced his retirement. The Giants tried to get Vince Lombardi to take his place, but Lombardi found a home in Green Bay. The Giants hired Allie Sherman instead. But the breeze of change turned into a full-fledged gust during that off-season when the Giants traded a young tackle named Lou Cordileone to the 49ers for veteran quarterback Y.A. Tittle. Plus, the Giants were going to have to run an offense without Frank Gifford, who had suffered a head injury from a hit by Chuck Bednarik during the 1960 season.

To help fill the gap, the Giants acquired Del Shofner, a receiver who'd played the first four years of his NFL career with the L.A. Rams. Tittle and Shofner were to turn into a magic combo. Tittle threw 'em, and Shofner caught 'em. All Tittle had to do was get it in the neighborhood, and Shofner's magic hands did the rest.

The Giants' defense, always tough, was back. The stars remained: Rosey Grier, Andy Robustelli, Jim Katcavage, and Sam

Y.A. Tittle breathed new life into the Giants when he replaced Charley Conerly at quarterback, leading the team to three consecutive championship games. (Photo courtesy of Getty Images)

Huff. At a time when many teams were losing talent to the competing American Football League, the Giants players had remained loyal to their team and their league. New to the defense was Erich Barnes (pronounced E-*rich*), a specialist in the fine art of the interception.

Running the ball for the Giants would be Alex Webster. Webster's 1960 season had been a nightmare, with holes closing left and right just before he reached them, but an off-season of conditioning paid off. Webster became the Giants' go-to guy when they needed to pound the ball and eat up clock. He carried the ball 196 times and gained 928 yards, a 4.7 yards-per-carry average.

When Tittle arrived at the Giants training camp for the first time during the summer of 1961, he was not greeted warmly by his new teammates. The team had been together for many years with little change in personnel, and the new quarterback, who had been a starter in the pros for 13 years already, was the writing on the wall. Charley Conerly's days as the Giants' quarterback were numbered.

The 40-year-old Conerly had had the job since 1948, and Tittle's arrival on the team was a reminder to everyone of their football mortality. Consequently, Tittle had to deal with the cold shoulder when he arrived.

Although Tittle, at 35 years old, was the younger of the two quarterbacks by five years, he looked older, mostly because he was bald. Drinking deeply from Yankee Stadium's fountain of youth, Tittle played like a young man despite his appearance. Among his new teammates there was agreement: he didn't look a day over 60.

Tittle was still filled with great joy to be in New York, despite his teammates' lack of hospitality. For years he had played on bad teams, and now he was on a contender, a team with a chance to go all the way, a team that had been holding itself back for a few years by—to be brutally honest—adapting itself to Conerly's advanced age.

The season started with Conerly and Tittle sharing the quarterback position, and both players were uncomfortable with the on-again, off-again feel of the arrangement. In the season opener,

Conerly started. He completed only nine passes for 75 yards, and the Giants lost to the Cards 21–10. Conerly looked even older than he had in 1960. Tittle waited on the sidelines, sensing that his time would come sooner rather than later.

Conerly also started the second game of the year, in Pittsburgh, and the Giants' offense looked leaden of foot out there. Giants fans were getting fidgety, anxious now for Coach Sherman to pull the trigger—and after halftime, he did. He pulled Conerly and put Tittle in the game.

Tittle went right to work. He threw a touchdown pass to Joe Morrison, and ol' reliable Pat Summerall kicked the game-winning field goal as the Giants prevailed 17–14.

It was somewhat of a surprise when Conerly started the third game of the season, against the Redskins in Washington, but this time Sherman was much quicker with the hook. By the end of the first quarter Tittle was in the game, and Tittle was the starter from that point on. Tittle took the helm with his team 14 points behind, and he brought the Giants back for the victory.

Conerly retired at the end of the season.

Certainly one of the biggest plays of the year for the Giants came during a game at the Cotton Bowl in Dallas against the expansion Cowboys. That big play came when Barnes intercepted a pass two yards deep in his own end zone and ran it back 102 yards for a touchdown.

Tittle's most famous pass of the 1961 season came in the ninth game of the year, on November 12, at Yankee Stadium, versus the Eagles. It was a battle for first place in the East, and it was a close, high-scoring game.

TIMELINE

That season, 1961, was the first in which the NFL played a 14-game schedule. It was also the year the Vikings, with Fran Tarkenton under center, and the Cowboys joined the league as expansion teams.

At one point, an Eagles blitz forced Tittle into scramble mode. To avoid a sack, Tittle heaved the ball in the direction of Kyle Rote down field. It would be an exaggeration to say the pass was end-over-end, but it sure wasn't a spiral. It looked as if he'd heaved up a loaf of Wonder Bread. The pass didn't have a heck of a lot of zip on it—there was a congregation of defenders surrounding Rote by the time the pigskin arrived. One defender batted the ball, but it went up rather than down. A second Eagle, now playing volleyball and diving to keep the ball from falling incomplete, batted the ball a second time, at which point Shofner grabbed it and ran into the end zone for a touchdown. That sunk the Eagles, who ended up losing by 17. The Giants took the lead in the division for keeps.

Tittle's performance during the regular season had been sufficient to earn him the league's MVP award. Sherman won Coach of the Year. Nine Giants were named to the Pro Bowl team.

For the 1961 NFL championship game the Giants traveled to City Stadium (now known as Lambeau Field) in Green Bay to face the Packers, who hadn't won a league championship in 17 years. It turned out to be a disappointing ending to a great season for the Giants. Packer Paul Hornung dominated the game, a game the Giants were never really in. The Giants only gained 130 yards on the day, as compared to the 345 yards the Packers racked up. Tittle didn't play well, throwing four interceptions.

Hornung, on the other hand, did a little bit of everything. He ran the ball, he caught the ball, he even kicked the ball. He tallied a record 19 points, scoring one touchdown and kicking three field goals.

After a scoreless first quarter, the Packers scored 24 points in the second quarter: on a six-yard touchdown run by Hornung, a 13-yard pass from Bart Starr to Boyd Dowler, a 14-yard pass from Starr to Ron Kramer, and a 17-yard field goal by Hornung.

Viewers could have turned off their TVs right then and not have missed anything, although the Packers did score 13 more points in the second half on two more Hornung field goals and another 13-yard touchdown pass from Starr to Kramer. The final score was 37–0, and though the drubbing was a bitter pill to

1961 NFL CHAMPIONSHIP GAME

City Stadium, Green Bay ,Wisconsin, December 31, 1961

	1	2	3	4	Total
Giants	0	0	0	0	0
Packers	0	24	10	3	37

Attendance: 39,029

swallow, Giants fans had reason to believe that their new quarterback had the team on the road to greater success.

1962: EVEN BETTER

The 1962 NFL season got off to a somber start. The Heisman Trophy winner, Ernie Davis out of Syracuse, had been drafted by Washington and then traded to the Browns, where he was to become the heir apparent to Jim Brown in the Cleveland backfield. But it wasn't to be. Tragically, Davis died of leukemia before he could make his NFL debut.

In the Giants organization, Conerly and Rote retired, although Rote was still around in his new capacity as assistant coach. On a positive note, Gifford was back, sufficiently recovered from his concussion and ready to resume his football career.

In 1962 Sherman played Gifford at flanker—his days as a ball carrier were through—and he was third on the team in pass receptions in 1962, behind only Shofner and Webster.

Just as had been the case the year before, the Giants lost their season opener, getting whomped by the Browns in Cleveland in front of more than 80,000 fans at Cleveland Municipal Stadium. Tittle threw three interceptions, and the Giants lost 17–7.

That was just a hiccup on the way to more greatness for Big Blue. The Giants won three in a row before playing their home opener in the fifth game of the season.

NEW YORK GIANTS

The 1962 New York Giants—a cast of characters that had been around for years. They were, from left to right: (Fifth Row) Assistant coach Ken Kavanaugh, Joe Walton, Andy Robustelli, Bob Simms, Jim Collier, Del Shofner, Jerry Hillebrand; (Fourth Row) Bob Hill, Charlie Janerette, Reed Bohovich, Jim Katcavage, Roosevelt "Rosey" Grier, Dick Modzelewski, Roosevelt Brown, Tom Scott; (Third Row) Assistant coach Ed Coleman, Greg Larson, Ray Wietecha, Ken Byers, Zeke Smith, Darrell Dess, Bookie Bolin, Mickey Walker, Jack Stroud, Sam Huff, assistant coach Kyle Rote; (Second Row) Alex Webster, Bill Winter, Don Chandler, Bob Gaiters, Joe Morrison, head coach Allie Sherman, Jim Podoley, Joe Taylor, Johnny Counts, Erich Barnes, Curtis Miranda; (First Row) Ralph Guglielmi, Y.A. Tittle, Frank Gifford, Francis Marriott, Jim Patton, Allan Webb, Dick Lynch, John Yaccino, Phil King, and Dick Pesonen.

The Giants had opened on the road for a month so as not to interfere with the Yankees, who played in yet another World Series that year. But once they were at home, the Giants failed to reward the faithful who had waited so long to see their team in person, losing to the Steelers 20–17.

Later, against the Lions, Tittle had to miss much of the first half. In a play that would surely result in a suspension today, Tittle was knocked out of action by a vicious hit that occurred well after he had crossed the goal line for a bootleg touchdown. Tittle returned in the second half and led the Giants to a 17–14 win.

The Giants did not lose another game for the remainder of the regular season, finishing with a nine-game winning streak. Stats show that Tittle's play got better during his second year with the club. He was, in fact, playing the best football of his career over a sustained period. It made some wonder what Tittle's career would have been like if he'd played all of it with a contender. In 1962 Tittle had an 89.5 quarterback rating. He passed for 3,224 yards, a personal best, and 33 touchdown passes, which was only two shy of the league record.

For Tittle the high point of the season, and perhaps the high point of his career, came against the Redskins at Yankee Stadium on October 28, 1962, when he passed for seven touchdowns. At one point during the game Tittle threw 12 consecutive completions, which was at the time one shy of the NFL record. Late in the game Tittle had opportunities to go for touchdown pass number eight, but the Giants, with a lead, handed the ball off instead in a show of good sportsmanship. Tittle finished that day with 27 completions in 39 attempts and a Giants-record 505 yards gained. That 505 was the team record until Phil Simms's air attack gained 513 during a game in 1985.

Although there were many new Giants fans around the country, brought on board by the NFL's exploding popularity as a Sunday afternoon television show, the fans who lived in the five boroughs were feeling frustrated. Only 65,000 fit in Yankee Stadium, but NFL rules prohibited broadcasting football in the home city. Games played in Yankee Stadium could be seen in Rochester, New York, but not in New York City. That rule was later changed, and TV broadcasts were only blacked out if the home team had failed to sell out its stadium. In 1962 it was even harder than usual for a Giants fan to keep tabs on his team because of a newspaper strike. Thank goodness for radio! Some home owners put special antennae on their roofs in an attempt to pick up the games on an out-of-town signal. The closest city that carried the blacked-out games was Hartford, Connecticut, on the other side of Long Island Sound.

Again the Giants finished first in the East, and again they played the Green Bay Packers in the NFL championship game.

JIM TAYLOR

In the 1962 NFL championship game, the Giants were defeated almost single-handedly by Packers running back Jim Taylor. That had been Taylor's best season. He led the league in rushing with 1,474 yards. Taylor's mark remains the Packers' team record for rushing yards in a season.

About the 1962 championship game, Taylor later recalled, "The game was played in some of the most severe conditions I've ever seen. There were cold, swirling winds, and the field itself was frozen over. The conditions were just brutal, the worst you could imagine. But to me, the conditions didn't matter. You simply had to go out and play in them and try to blank out everything else. You had to do what you could with the weather and keep going. Was a good thing I had that kind of mentality because I got the ball a lot that day, running it 31 times for the Green Bay Packers against the New York Giants' defense. By the end of the game, I was pretty beat up. I had stitches put into my arm at halftime: I think I had about six of them. I kept scraping the wound open every time I hit the ground because it was so frozen and hard. I'd also bitten my tongue, and that was bleeding pretty good, too. It was so cold—probably about 25 below zero with the wind chill—that ice was forming around the players' eyelids and noses. Yankee Stadium was a little tough to play in because it obviously was designed for baseball. As a result, there were areas of the infield where there was no grass. Those places would get frozen up quickly and feel as hard as a rock when you got tackled on them."

This year, however, the game was played in Yankee Stadium in front of a full house of screaming Giants fans.

The weather was horrible. The temperature was in the teens, and the wind was whipping up to 40 miles per hour, bound to play havoc with the Giants' aerial attack.

This was no drubbing; it was a tough, close, defensive game, but in the long run, the result was the same. The Packers popped open the champagne bottles, and the Giants hung their heads and told reporters to just wait 'til next year.

The Giants actually gained more yards than the Packers had in the 1962 championship game—291 to 244—but that's not how they keep score. The Packers' scoring came on three Jerry Kramer field goals, from 26, 29, and 30 yards, and one touchdown in the second quarter on a seven-yard Jim Taylor run. Kramer hit one field goal apiece in the first, third, and fourth quarters. Taylor's touchdown came in the second quarter, following a short drive set up by Giants fullback Phil King's fumble.

The Giants' offense gained yards but couldn't finish off drives. The Packers' defense would bend a little each time the Giants had the ball, then stiffen before New York had a chance to score points. The Giants' only score of the game came on special teams in the third quarter, when Barnes blocked a Max McGee punt deep in Packers territory and the Giants' Jim Collier covered it for a touchdown.

For the fourth time in five years the Giants had made it as far as the NFL championship game but had come away without a championship. For the second year in a row the Giants' offense had powered the team to the brink of supremacy but then buckled and come up scoreless in the final game.

All of the kicking for the Giants was being done by Don Chandler. Summerall had made the easy conversion from football player to sports announcer. In 1962 Chandler set the Giants record with 104 points. He would break his own record by scoring 106 points in 1963, the following season.

1962 NFL CHAMPIONSHIP GAME

Yankee Stadium, Bronx, N.Y., December 30, 1962

	1	2	3	4	Total
Packers	3	7	3	3	16
Giants	0	0	7	0	7

Attendance: 64,892

Robustelli extended his own record for career fumble recoveries. He now had 21. Eight of those came as a Giant, with the first 13 for the L.A. Rams.

1963: BEST EVER

Heading into the 1963 season, some football analysts predicted a downturn for New York. Some said the team had hung onto its veterans too long, that the young talent coming in wasn't sufficient to replace the flood of talent that, having served well, was on its way out.

But the season began well for Big Blue. For the first time in three years the Giants won their season opener, 37–28, over the Colts in Baltimore, with Tittle throwing three touchdown passes. The quarterback, however, suffered injured ribs on a hit in the third quarter, an injury so severe that it kept him out of the remainder of that game and the next game in Pittsburgh.

The Giants did not fare well without Tittle and lost 31–0 to the Steelers in the season's second game. Then Tittle returned, and the Giants beat Philadelphia and Washington before playing their home opener—again delayed because the Yankees were in the World Series—against the Browns.

Jim Brown ran all over the Giants that day, and the undefeated Browns went to 5–0 with a 34–24 victory over the Giants at Yankee Stadium. The Giants dropped to 3–2, and there were renewed grumblings from the Giants-are-old contingent.

The Giants perked up at that point, however, especially the offense, scoring almost 40 points per game from then on. The most satisfying victory during this stretch came when New York visited Cleveland and beat the Browns 33–6. Jim Brown, so dominant during the teams' first meeting of the season, was held to only 40 yards on the ground and was ejected in the fourth quarter for fighting.

The 1963 season was marked by the assassination of President John F. Kennedy in Dallas on November 22. Commissioner Pete Rozelle made the controversial decision to play the NFL schedule as planned on November 24. On that day—with no one watching the games, so riveted were they by the murder of Lee Harvey Oswald live on national TV—the Giants were defeated by the Cardinals in Yankee Stadium. It was the Giants' last defeat of the regular season. They finished the season 11–3, one game ahead of Cleveland.

Tittle's performance, incredibly enough, improved yet again for the 1963 season. His quarterback rating again rose, this time to 104.8. He set the NFL record with 36 touchdown passes. He also completed more than 60 percent of his passes, leading the league in that category. Tittle also led the league by gaining more than eight and a half yards per passing attempt. His performance that year was especially impressive because he played with an injured knee. Hobbled and unable to scramble, he needed lots of protection from his front line, and he got it. Tittle's 36 touchdown passes in the 1963 season would remain an NFL record until Dan Marino threw 48 touchdown passes in 1984.

In the 1963 NFL championship game, Tittle's knee was barely supporting his weight, and it took all of his skills just to drop back into the pocket. The Western Division champions that year were the Chicago Bears, and the championship game was played at Wrigley Field in Chicago. The Bears were in their first NFL championship game since 1956, when they lost to the Giants. While the 1963 Giants had a potent offense and a suspect defense, the Bears were the other way around, and it was their menacing defense that had given them the best record in the west. The

1963 NFL CHAMPIONSHIP GAME

Wrigley Field, Chicago, Illinois, December 29, 1963

	1	2	3	4	Total
Giants	7	3	0	0	10
Bears	7	0	7	0	14

Attendance: 45,801

championship game would feature the best passing offense in the league against the best passing defense.

The pain in Tittle's knee—not helped by the harsh cold and windy conditions, an NFL championship game tradition—affected his accuracy, and he was intercepted five times. It's hard for a team to win a game when the quarterback is completing almost as many passes to his opponents as he is to his own receivers. The Bears, as it turned out, scored *all* of their points off interceptions.

It was the Giants' third consecutive NFL championship game, and, in the first quarter, they did something they hadn't done before during that streak: they took the lead. In the first quarter, Tittle led the Giants down the field 83 yards, finishing with a 14-yard touchdown pass to Gifford. That was more like it, Giants fans said to themselves. For years now they had watched a team that had played great during the regular season but couldn't finish the deal in the final game of the year.

Maybe this time the story would be different. Early optimism only grew when, still in the first quarter, Bears halfback Willie Galimore fumbled at the Bears' 31, and the Giants recovered the ball.

The Giants looked sure to take a commanding lead when Tittle found Shofner open in the Bears' end zone. Shofner was famous for his great hands and usually only needed to get one hand on the ball to catch it. Tittle hit him right in those hands for a seemingly easy touchdown, but Shofner inexplicably dropped the ball. The Giants came away empty.

The next time the Giants had the ball, fans' optimism dimmed even further. Tittle threw one of his devastating interceptions, this one to Bear Larry Morris, who saw the screen pass coming as if he had been in the Giants huddle. Morris ran the ball back to the Giants' 5. Two plays later, Bears quarterback Billy Wade took the ball in himself from two yards out to even the score.

The Giants took a three-point lead into halftime when punter-turned-place-kicker Don Chandler kicked a 13-yard field goal. (In this day and age, with the goal posts on the back line of the end zone, a 13-yard field goal would be impossibly short, but back in 1963 the goal posts were right on the goal line. Extra points were kicked from only seven or eight yards away.

The Giants' offense was again shut down, and New York failed to score in the second half. The winning touchdown came in the third quarter, and again it was a direct result of an interception, again on a screen pass.

This time it was Bears defensive end Ed O'Bradovich who made the pick, returning the ball to the Giants' 14. Another quarterback sneak by Wade five plays later from one yard out gave the Bears the 14–10 lead, which turned out to be the final score. As the final seconds ticked down, Tittle could be seen on the Giants' sideline wrapped in a parka, tears streaming down his face.

Three straight years the Giants made it to the championship game, and three times they were denied, yet Giants fans do not look back on those years as years of anguish. Hardly. The 23 years that followed, before the Giants were again in a championship game, many of them when the Giants were just flat-out bad— *those* were seasons of anguish.

The 1961–63 streak is considered a classic period for the Giants. They won three consecutive division championships with a cast of characters that had been around for years. The big difference was that Tittle had taken over as quarterback.

UPS AND DOWNS

This chapter is a mixed bag of good and bad, the beautiful and the butt-ugly. In our first story the Giants show grit and determination. In the second story they fold like the back cover of *Mad* magazine.

21 POINTS IN THE FOURTH QUARTER

In order for any comeback to take place, a team has to fall into a deficit, which is just what the Giants did at Yankee Stadium on November 15, 1970, in a game against the Redskins. After starting the season with three straight losses, the Giants were looking for their sixth straight victory, but it didn't look good when the Redskins scored three touchdowns in the third quarter to take a 33–14 lead. That score remained until the 10-minute mark of the fourth quarter.

The Giants' defense, which had been vulnerable to both Sonny Jurgensen's passes and Charlie Harraway's runs in the third quarter, held tough in the fourth quarter, allowing Giants quarterback Fran Tarkenton to work his magic. The scoring didn't come on long plays but rather on long drives. The three touchdowns the Giants scored in the fourth quarter came on drives of 71, 65, and 73 yards. The Giants pretty much had the ball for the entire fourth quarter. The Redskins managed no first downs. They punted the ball twice and once gave it up on downs.

The first scoring drive for the Giants started during the last seconds of the third quarter and ended, five minutes deep into the fourth quarter, with a five-yard run by Ron Johnson. Tarkenton's arm had taken the Giants down the field, with 60 of the 71 yards gained coming through the air. The Redskins went three and out, and the Giants came right back down the field. The second drive only took two plays, both passes to Tucker Frederickson. The second was caught at the 30, and Frederickson ran it the rest of the way in. Another three-and-out by the Redskins, and the Giants had the ball with a chance to take the lead. A little more than four minutes were left on the clock. Bobby Duhon returned the Redskins punt from the 6 to the 27. On the first play from scrimmage, Tarkenton threw a bullet to Bob Tucker for 20 yards. Another completion to Frederickson took the ball to the Redskins' 32-yard line at the two-minute warning. After the break, the Giants temporarily stalled and found themselves with a fourth-and-6 at the Redskins' 28.

"He [Tarkenton] asked me if could I beat the guy," Johnson recalled years later. "I said, 'You're damn right I can beat him.' So that's basically what happened. He had the faith in me that I could get open. When people have that kind of faith in you, you can't let them down. That's the great thing about football...it's a team game, and everybody did what they had to do."

Tarkenton completed a short pass to Johnson at the 18 for the first down. One more completion took the ball to the nine, and from there Johnson ran it in around the left end for the winning touchdown.

"I was just wide open to run that in," Johnson said. "Everybody did what they had to do on that one. [Frederickson] blocked his butt off for me. He was like a big brother. I remember [Dick] Butkus and I got into it once, and he came over like a madman. He said, 'Don't you mess with this kid.'"

Tarkenton finished the game with 320 yards passing.

When the game was over, Giants head coach Alex Webster was still huffing and puffing with excitement. The coach told the press, "What makes you feel proud is the way they wouldn't give up. This is what you try to get from them, to make them believe

On November 15, 1970, quarterback Fran Tarkenton led the Giants on three long touchdown drives in the fourth quarter to stun the Redskins. (Photo courtesy of Bettmann/Corbis)

in themselves. When the last quarter was starting, I kept telling them that Washington had gotten three quick scores and we could turn around and do exactly the same—if the defense would get us the ball."

Years later Johnson recalled the scene in the winning locker room, saying, "It was crazy. It was a great, great victory. With the Giants not having great teams prior to that, it was just such a great feeling to be part of that. I remember we just went crazy after that game. The big thing is that, as I mentioned, we had a lot of new players, and we all bonded together so well. It took us a couple of games to get bonded, but after that, we felt we could beat anybody. It was just a real great feeling."

Frederickson remembered it too, saying, "I remember we had a big party after the game. We always did, but we had a better one that night. Everyone used to come over to my apartment [in Manhattan] after the game, and it was good times. It was a good bunch of guys. The chemistry was great with that group, and Alex was a great guy—is a great guy. I just remember we had a big time afterward."

One of the best things about the Giants' miracle comeback in 1970 was that it gave Frederickson a chance to be a hero. He caught 10 passes during the game and scored two touchdowns. Frederickson had been often injured and often overshadowed during his time with the Giants. He'd played for the Giants since the mid-1960s and was the last of a breed. A soft-spoken man who had been called "a football player's football player," he'd been a star at Auburn University, where he played both offense and defense.

Maybe you've heard your grandfather tell of a time when men were men and football clubs only had 11 members. Everybody played both ways the entire game. Well, little by little, the game became specialized and more brutal. The pads got bigger, and each player appeared on the field less. And Frederickson was the last guy who never wanted out of the game.

On offense at Auburn he was a running back, and he averaged 4.4 yards per carry during his senior year in 1964. On defense he was listed as a safety, but he often crowded the line of scrimmage until he was practically positioned as a lineman by the time the ball was snapped. He was known to tackle opposing players for a loss. He led the 1963 Auburn team in interceptions with four as a junior.

He was born in Hollywood, Florida, and attended South Broward High School. He grew to be 6'2", and his running weight was a lean, mean 210 pounds. In both his junior and senior years he won the Jacobs Award as the best-blocking back in the Southeastern Conference. In 1992 Auburn held a poll to determine the school's All-Century Team, and Frederickson was the top vote-getter. As a senior he was named both first-team All-American and conference MVP. He graduated from Auburn with a degree in science.

He was a Giant from 1965 until 1971, when a knee injury ended his career. Although he did return a few kicks and caught a pass for every five times he ran with the ball, he didn't play defense. His days of playing both ways were over.

During his days as a player he continued to study—finance this time—and even before he retired from the gridiron he was moonlighting as an investment broker for the firm of Allen & Co. After football he worked for that company full-time and was eventually promoted to vice president for investment banking.

Thirty-six years after the comeback against the Redskins, Frederickson was asked by a reporter if he remembered the game. He did. He said, "Fran was dinking [throwing short passes] to me all day. That was sort of the game plan, and it started working, and Franny just kept going to me. I got loose on one of them and scored. I still have the game ball—it's sitting in my house. That was fun. That was a good game. Sam Huff was on that Redskins team. I had some good friends on that team, and those guys were yelling at me. We got it going, and they were moaning, believe me. That was a great year. Everybody, everything was clicking, and we had it going. We had a chemistry that you could never describe on paper. I don't think we were as good as we played, but we certainly had it going."

Ron Johnson remembered it too, saying, "Fran Tarkenton was one of the best leaders I've ever played with in my lifetime. He was a magician. That team had [wide receiver] Clifton McNeil, but Clifton had a big, huge ego. We had Bob Tucker, who was a great, great tight end, and Donnie Herrmann and Rich Houston. We felt that we could play with anybody and do whatever we

ON THE MOVE

During the so-called "bleak years," the Giants stopped playing in Yankee Stadium. The move was necessitated by a two-year refurbishment of the big ballpark in the Bronx. During that time the Giants played at the Yale Bowl in Connecticut. And, although many Giants fans remained faithful and made the trek up to New Haven for home games, they didn't like it. After spending 1973 and 1974 in the Yale Bowl and 1975 in Shea Stadium in Queens, New York, the Giants moved once again, this time to their state-of-the-art new facility, Giants Stadium in New Jersey. The new stadium cost $78 million to build and had a seating capacity of 78,741.

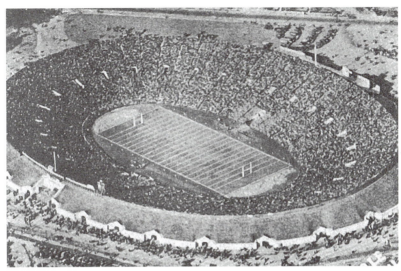

In 1974, between their stays at Yankee Stadium and Giants Stadium, Big Blue played home games at the Yale Bowl in Connecticut, which meant a looooong road trip for New York fans who wanted to cheer on their heroes in person.

Giants Stadium in New Jersey has been the team's home since 1976. The Jets became co-tenants in 1984.

needed to do. It was just all great stuff. It was a team made up of a lot of new, first-year players—it was not an old Giants team, I guess is where I'm going. We all just sort of meshed together, and I remember we had lost our first couple of games, and then we went on a roll."

Eight days after the great comeback game versus the Redskins, the Giants went to Philadelphia and lost on a Monday night. After that they won three in a row and went into the final game of the year, at home, needing a victory over the Rams to make the play-offs. But they lost 31–3 and that was that. Still, the 1970 Giants managed to give their fans something they weren't used to at that time: a winning season.

BLOWING A 24-POINT LEAD TO THE 49ERS

It was only a few years back, and the pain is still real, the wounds deep. The Giants had the 49ers trounced in their playoff game on January 5, 2003, and then collapsed like a house of cards.

The biggest comeback in NFL playoff history was a 32-pointer by Buffalo in a 41–38 win over the Houston Oilers in January 1993. But this was the second biggest. And the Giants were the victims, the 49ers the victors.

Incredibly, the Giants were winning the game 38–14 in the third quarter. Candlestick Park in San Francisco was hushed. Fans were starting to leave. It clearly wasn't going to be the 49ers' day. But wait....

When the tide turned, it really turned, and from that point on, the 49ers could do no wrong—and the Giants could do no right. The only enemy the 49ers had was the clock, and the only question was whether or not the Giants were going to have enough time to stage a comeback of their own.

According to legend, the 49ers were inspired to make their historic postseason comeback by that leader amongst men, Terrell Owens, who was overheard in the 49ers locker room saying, "Are we pretenders or contenders? We're either going to pretend, or we're going to contend. It's time to decide. We have a lot of weapons. We have to play with poise. Time is on our side."

The 49ers' Chike Okeafor (foreground) lies on the ground after breaking up a pass thrown by Giants snapper Matt Allen in the final minutes of the NFC Wild Card game in San Francisco on January 5, 2003, while the Giants' Marcellus Rivers (83) and Rich Seubert (69) gesture at left for an interference call. The NFL admitted the next day that a penalty should have been called against the 49ers on the final play of the 39–38 Giants loss.

With four minutes left in the third quarter, the Giants led 38–14. The 49ers, deciding to be contenders because T.O. said so, scored 25 consecutive points. The first 22 came on three touchdowns on consecutive possessions, one on a Jeff Garcia bootleg and two on touchdown passes. All three times the 49ers tried for the two-point conversion, and they succeeded twice, both on passes from Garcia to Owens.

The Giants' collapse became complete when, with one minute left, the 49ers scored on a 13-yard touchdown pass from Garcia to Tai Streets. The 49ers took a one-point lead.

The Giants had looked spectacular in the first half. Three times quarterback Kerry Collins had thrown touchdown passes to Toomer. But the Giants' offense lost its mojo at halftime, just as the 49ers were finding theirs.

And somehow this game found a way to be even more cruel than just a collapse, because even with all that had gone wrong, the Giants found themselves with a chance to win it in the last seconds, a chance that was squandered with a hideous comedy of errors.

There were six seconds left on the clock. The Giants lined up for a 41-yard field goal attempt. The Giants' holder, Matt Allen, fumbled the snap and then panicked. He heaved up the ball in the general direction of offensive lineman Rich Seubert. While the ball was on its way, Seubert was yanked to the turf at the 4-yard line by 49ers defensive end Chike Okeafor for apparent pass interference. The ball fell harmlessly to the ground. The clock read zero. The referees said there was a flag on the play, but it was against the Giants for an illegal receiver downfield—a typical call on kicking plays that fall apart. The refs ruled the game over and the 49ers the victors, 39–38. When the referee was asked after the game why no pass interference was called, he said it wasn't pass interference if the receiver was ineligible. Except, it was pointed out, the illegal receiver downfield was left guard Tam Hopkins and the intended receiver was Seubert, who had lined up as an eligible receiver.

"There was so much commotion at the end that there was nothing I could do about it. I couldn't challenge it. I couldn't do anything," coach Jim Fassel said. That made Giants fans grind their teeth.

Some Giants fans said that the pass interference call wouldn't have been necessary if Allen had done the right thing. Instead of actually trying to score with a desperation move, he should have realized that it was only third down. Once he ran out of the pocket—thus eliminating the possibility of an intentional grounding penalty—all he had to do was fling the ball out of bounds to stop the clock.

Giants fans looking for a goat mostly blamed Allen, but those more creative in their thinking blamed the Giants' flamboyant rookie tight end Jeremy Shockey, who—though making seven catches for 68 yards during the game—dropped the one that mattered most. Shockey couldn't keep his mitts on a sure touchdown pass in the third quarter, and the Giants had to settle for a field goal. Those additional four points, some fans figured, would have been the deciding factor in the game.

Losing that way is always tough, but losing to T.O. made it worse. His strutting and incessant taunting made losing a bitter thing. The trouble was, T.O. backed it all up on the field, catching pass after pass and even throwing a completion on an option play that gave the 49ers first and goal at the Giants' 1. It was Owens's first pass attempt of the season.

A few days after the game, depressed Giants fans were turned into full-fledged suicide risks when the NFL publicly stated that the refs had made a mistake on the last play of the collapse. A pass-interference penalty should have been called against the 49ers at the end of the game. The refs correctly called New York for an ineligible receiver downfield but failed to call pass interference on the 49ers when receiver Seubert was tackled as he tried to catch the pass that followed the Giants' bungled field-goal attempt. The correct call, the NFL admitted, was off-setting penalties and a do-over—so the Giants would have gotten a second chance to kick the game-winning field goal. Though it was true that time ran out during the final play, NFL rules dictate that the game cannot end on off-setting penalties.

BOOM! OUT GO THE LIGHTS

In football it's called getting one's bell rung. In medical terms, it's a severe concussion, a bruise to the brain, and it can make you feel crummy for years. Here's the story of a couple of Giants greats who got their bells rung.

CHUCK BEDNARIK "KILLS" FRANK GIFFORD

Chuck Bednarik's hit on Frank Gifford at Yankee Stadium on November 20, 1960, was named by Kevin Hench of FOXSports.com on October 24, 2006, as the "most devastating hit" in sports history. (Jack Tatum tattooing Sammy White in Super Bowl XI was number two.)

Bednarik once described the play as "a Volkswagen going down a one-way street the wrong way, and a Mack truck is coming the opposite way. Frank was doing a down-and-in pattern, and I saw him coming. I just hit him high in the chest about as hard as I could. His head snapped, and he went flying one way and the ball went flying another."

Giants linebacker Sam Huff, who watched the hit up close and in person, commented, "I thought Bednarik killed him." Gifford lay on the field like a rag doll, and despite urgent efforts by the increasingly concerned team doctor, he wasn't waking up.

The man lying so still on the ground was not just any football player. Gifford was born August 16, 1930, in Santa Monica,

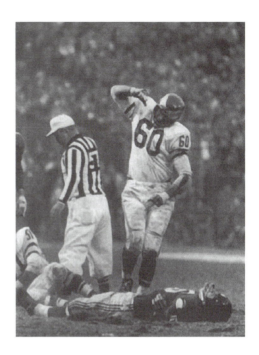

Despite appearances, Chuck Bednarik claims he didn't know Frank Gifford had been injured when he celebrated. The only thing on his mind was his teammate recovering Gifford's fumble.

California, and was the biggest football star New York had ever known. Not only was he the best year after year at a multitude of football skills, but he had the looks of a movie star. He was Frank Gifford, and his name was already synonymous with football by the time he became the Giants' number-one draft pick in 1952. Gifford's fame started when he was a teenager, a high school phenom. Much like O.J. Simpson years later, he was a household name by the time he enrolled in college. And, again like O.J., that college was the University of Southern California. At USC Gifford played both offense and defense, and as a senior he was named All-American.

When Gifford arrived in New York from the West Coast in 1952, he could do it all. Giants head coach Steve Owen had thought he needed a number of players to make his team jell, but now he wasn't so sure. He was starting to think he only needed one player, that Gifford encompassed all of his missing parts.

Gifford could run, pass, catch, play defensive back, and return kicks. In 1953, in a time when it was routine to use mutually exclusive squads for offense and defense, Gifford still played on both sides of the ball. In his second year in the NFL Gifford averaged an otherworldly 50 minutes per game. He probably would have performed with the band at halftime, too, if they'd let him. Gifford was the league MVP in 1956, a Giants championship year. He ran with the ball, caught passes, threw passes, and even kicked a field goal.

Now, in 1960, against the Eagles, lying there on the torn earth, he looked dead. After some time was spent trying to resuscitate Gifford on the field, he was placed on a stretcher and taken off. With a solemn quietness, the game resumed without him.

Little did the Giants know that at that very moment, even as Gifford continued to snooze, a policeman on the field had suffered a heart attack. A second medical emergency had arisen, this one tragic, as the man died before he could be transported from his post. He was placed on a stretcher and carried to a tunnel under the stadium, where he was placed on a gurney until an ambulance could arrive to take him away. When the gun blew to announce the end of the game, the Giants had to go through that same tunnel to get to their clubhouse. They walked right by the body which, by this time, had a sheet pulled all the way up over its head. Naturally, they assumed that it was Gifford. Players were devastated in the locker room. The team dedicated the rest of the season to its dearly departed leader. It wasn't until later that the players learned that Gifford, although in bad shape, had lived. A complete stranger was under the sheet. In fact, the heart-attack victim's body had been left in the tunnel for so long because Gifford's emergency had commandeered the first ambulance that was called, and a second ambulance had to be called to transport the heart-attack victim to the morgue.

In the next day's paper there was a photo of the vicious hit, which today remains one of the most famous football photos ever. Gifford, of course, can be seen doing his corpse impression, while Bednarik leaps for joy and pumps his fist. When published in the next day's paper, the photo caused a bit of an outrage. It looked like Bednarik, having killed the football hero, was celebrating the moment. Bednarik couldn't stop telling people how wrong they were.

Even 40 years later at autograph shows, Bednarik knows which photo everyone is going to want him to sign, and he knows that every autograph-seeker will ask why he was so happy that he'd killed Gifford. So, if his response sounds a little bit rote, take into consideration he has been asked this question before, once or twice: "After I hit him my eyes were following the ball. I didn't know where Frank had gone. One of our linebackers, Chuck Weber, was scrambling to get the ball. Look at the photo. My eyes were closed, and my fists were clenched. And I just happened to turn around so that I'm facing Gifford and the photographer. It was unbeknownst to me that Gifford was lying there on the ground, unconscious. I had no idea he was there."

Bednarik notes that there was another photo, taken right after the first one, in which he's crouching down in concern, checking to see if Gifford was, you know, still breathing—but no one cares about that photo.

Someone once asked Bednarik what he was saying at the instant the famous photo was taken, and he replied, censoring himself, "I said, 'This f'ing game is over!'"

Bednarik was a bit of a throwback, just like Gifford. He was the team's starting center, but when linebacker Bob Pellegrini was injured, Bednarik took over that job as well. For nine games that season, Bednarik appeared in every play from scrimmage, regardless of who had the ball.

As it turned out, Gifford's concussion may have cost the Giants a shot at the championship game that year. Gifford was such a big part of the Giants' offense, after all. The team was 5–2–1 when Gifford lost consciousness. They were 1–2–1 the rest of the way, finishing 6–4–2, third place in the NFL East.

Gifford missed the remainder of that season and all of the next one, but he didn't want his career to end on that ugly note. Some warriors might have been satisfied being carried off the field on their shield, but not Gifford. He returned for three more seasons as a flanker, catching passes for the last seasons of the Giants' glory years.

Said Gifford, "I was out the rest of the year and decided to quit. Then, in early 1961, I started thinking about how much I would miss the game. I went to talk about it with Toots [Shor]. He reminded me of what I had already accomplished and how much I owed it to myself to see that I really was finished. I took his advice, came back, and went on for several more years, including a couple of Pro Bowl teams."

Gifford was selected to eight Pro Bowl teams at three different positions. Six times he was named first- or second-team All-NFL. He gained almost 10,000 all-purpose yards in the NFL.

After football Gifford had another Hall of Fame career as a sportscaster, working for CBS Sports as the anchor of their pregame show for many years before becoming the longtime play-by-play and color commentator for ABC's *Monday Night Football*.

THE BLEEDING ICON

It was September 20, 1964, and the Giants were playing the Steelers at old Pitt Stadium. Y.A. Tittle, the bald veteran who'd led the Giants to three consecutive NFL championship games and who had, the previous year, set the record for most touchdown passes in a season with 36, grew old on a single play. Ugly, indeed.

Tittle dropped back to pass to Gifford, but just as he was about to release the ball, he was clotheslined by Steelers defensive end John Baker. The ball popped up into the air and Tittle's helmet flew off, a combination that led some horrified spectators to believe Tittle had been decapitated by the blow.

In the mayhem, the Steelers grabbed the ball and scored a touchdown. Tittle, suffering from a deep concussion, knelt motionless in his own end zone, blood dripping down his face from a cut atop his hairless scalp.

He had reinjured his ribs on the play as well and was having trouble breathing, feeling a stabbing pain in his chest each time he tried to inhale. That moment, caught on film, has become a well-known symbol of the "agony of defeat." Tittle, who had a 104.8 quarterback rating in 1963, dropped to a 51.6 rating the following season, his last.

Y.A. Tittle's career didn't end when Steelers defensive end John Baker hit him and knocked his helmet off in Pitt Stadium on September 20, 1964, but it was the end of Tittle's days as an NFL superstar.

Tittle was suddenly so old. He'd been a wonder, the only bald guy on the team—completely bald, only a rim of hair—and he'd been so great, throwing touchdown passes in record numbers and leading the Giants to three consecutive NFL championship games. Wonderful, wonderful—and now, in the blink of an eye, with one savage blow to the head—old.

But many still recalled how it had not always been so, how Tittle once had been young. Yelberton Abraham Tittle had been a star quarterback at LSU, then went to the pros and into the All-

TITTLE FUN FACTS

During his pro career, Tittle completed 2,427 passes for 33,070 yards and 242 touchdowns. He threw for more than 300 yards in 13 games, quite a feat in that era. He threw 33 touchdown passes in 1962 and 36 in 1963. He won the NFL MVP award in 1961 and 1963 and was elected to seven Pro Bowls. Born October 24, 1926, in Marshall, Texas, he was almost 38 years old as he knelt in the end zone bleeding from the head.

THE PHOTO

The moment was memorialized in several photos. Every photographer in the stadium took a picture of the fallen quarterback. But one photo in particular captured the essence of the moment better than the others. That was the photo taken by Morris Berman of the *Pittsburgh Post-Gazette*.

According to Greg Garneau, executive director of the National Press Photographers Association, Berman's photo editor "wouldn't run the picture in the newspaper because it didn't have any action in it."

The photo ended up winning the National Headliner Award for Best Sports Photograph in 1964. Today the original print of that photo hangs on the wall of the Hall of Fame in Canton, Ohio. It is one of football's iconic images.

According to historians of photojournalism, Berman's photo influenced all sports photography that followed. Photographers quickly learned that the human drama at a sporting event was not limited to game action.

This was not the first time that Berman had taken a famous photograph—as an Army photographer in Europe during World War II, his best-known images were of the corpses of Italian dictator Benito Mussolini and his mistress. Berman died in 2007 at the age of 92.

American Football Conference. He played for the Baltimore Colts, first in the AAFC and then in the NFL from 1948 to 1950. With a quarterback rating higher than 90, Tittle was the AAFC Rookie of the Year in 1948.

From 1951 to 1960 Tittle quarterbacked the San Francisco 49ers, and it was at the tail end of his career that he came to New York and had his most memorable performances. At 6'0", 192 pounds, Tittle was small by today's standards, but big enough at the time. Still, one of the moves he perfected as a younger quarterback was the jump pass, in which he would jump as high as he could, like a basketball player, to better pass over charging defenders. Used during a screen pass, it allowed Tittle to wait longer before releasing the ball and led to many successful completions.

Today, the stories of Tittle's end zone kneel have been exaggerated. They say it was the final game of his career, but that's not true. He played a full season in 1964; he just didn't play well. The 1963 Giants had gone to the NFL championship game. The 1964 version won only two games, finishing the year 2–10–2.

The hit on Tittle came in only the second game of the year, and, truth be told, things didn't look that great for the Giants even before Tittle got his bell rung. New York lost its season opener at Philadelphia, 38–7. The next game, in Pittsburgh, was a close affair, and the Giants were in it right to the end, but they fell, as did their quarterback. The final score was 27–24—Steelers 1, Tittle 0. In the third week of the year, the Giants won their home opener at Yankee Stadium, beating the Redskins 13–10 without Tittle. A bad loss in Detroit and a tie with the Cowboys followed. Tittle returned for the game against the newfangled Cowboys, but he was not the same. And he would never be the same again. In their two games against the Cardinals that year they won one and tied one, but they lost all of their other games. Thus began the infamous two decades of bad football.

The decline of the Giants was not all Tittle's fault. The Giants' defense, already exhibiting porousness in 1963, developed gaping holes in 1964 and allowed 399 points.

At the end of the two-win season, Tittle, Gifford, and Webster all announced their retirements—and the bleak years had officially arrived.

TITTLE TODAY

Y.A. Tittle has been married to the same woman for more than 50 years, the former Minnette Deloach. After football, Tittle started his own still-thriving insurance business. Because NFL wages were what they were, the quarterback had worked during his off-seasons as a door-to-door insurance salesman, so going into the insurance business seemed like a natural choice when he retired from football. In 1995, Tittle's daughter Dianne Tittle de Laet wrote a book about her father called *Giants and Heroes*.

MODERN TIMES

ere are a couple of stories about the recent past. One's about a great running back in Giants history, and the other's about the painful Jekyll-and-Hyde feeling fans got watching the 2006 Giants win and lose and win and lose.

THE 2006 MELTDOWN

The Giants were playing the Bears on a rainy Sunday night at Giants Stadium on November 12, 2006. Both teams had excellent records, and the game had been publicized as the game of the week. During the first half the Giants were in control. As sheets of rain flowed down, the Giants dominated the line of scrimmage. Tiki Barber was running easily through the big holes and elusively through the small ones, and, on defense, the Giants were swarming like a gang of Lawrence Taylors. But, despite the dominance, the Giants only led 13–3 with less than a minute to play in the first half.

Then the momentum changed. Up until that point the Bears had been able to accumulate only 52 yards of offense, but on the next play quarterback Rex Grossman handed the ball off to Thomas Jones on a draw play, and Jones ran for 26 yards. Three plays later the Bears scored to pull within three points. That was the beginning of 21 straight points by the Bears.

Still, the Giants hung in there, despite a less-than-stellar effort from Eli Manning, who was more successful throwing the ball to the guys in the white shirts than he was to those in the blue. Manning also fumbled three times, mostly because his arm was being smacked by defenders as he tried to throw, and one of those fumbles resulted in another turnover.

In the fourth quarter the Bears led by just four points, this despite the fact that Giants left tackle Luke Petigout had to leave the game in the first quarter with a broken tibia and defensive starters Michael Strahan and Osi Umenyiora were already watching from the sideline because of injuries.

When a Giants drive stalled near the Bears' 35-yard line, coach Tom Coughlin sent field-goal kicker Jay Feely into the game. Although the rain had stopped by this time, the wind was still whipping. All of the field goals in the game had been kicked in the same direction, and it wasn't the direction the Giants were headed. Feely had already missed a 33-yarder in that direction—and this attempt was to be from 52 yards. Feely got the kick up high and straight, but in the wind, it didn't quite have the oomph to make it over the crossbar. It fell two yards short, where it was caught near the back of the Bears' end zone by Devin Hester. Hester was a backup cornerback who had wandered quietly into his own end zone just in case the kick was short. He held the ball loosely and stood still for an excruciatingly long second or two, looking as if he were about to take a knee and down the ball. The Giants slowed up, relaxed, and apparently thought of other things. It was then that Hester began to run, heading for the right sideline. He picked up blockers and remained untouched for the next 108 yards, scoring the Bears touchdown that put the final nail into the Giants' coffin. The play tied the longest in NFL history. The record can be broken, but not by much—the longest possible play is 109.99999 yards.

Hester went on to have the greatest all-time year in terms of returning different types of kicks for touchdowns. His Bears went to the Super Bowl in Miami, where Hester ran the opening kickoff back for a touchdown, the only time that had ever happened in Super Bowl history.

The final score of this game was 38–20 Bears. Chicago had scored 35 of the game's final 42 points, not bad after being pushed around in the rain for most of the first half—but very bad for Big Blue.

After the game a clearly frustrated Jeremy Shockey spoke with the *New York Post*. As a play-making tight end, Shockey was a guy who helped make the offense go, but he'd only caught one pass in the loss to the Bears. He said, "The best thing about playing football is that it is a team sport. As a team, we practice together, we travel together, we lift weights together, we run together, we rehab together, we eat together, we watch film together, we socialize together. That means we win and lose as a unit. We share the highs and the lows. We celebrate and commiserate with each other. We form a brotherhood with friendships and memories that can last a lifetime. It's a special feeling that we all share as part of the same team. Football is a team sport, no doubt about it. But every player on the field has to fight his own individual battles. We have to be able to count on each other to have each other's backs. To say that I walked off that field against the Bears unhappy is an outrageous understatement."

Next along the meltdown trail was the Titanic Choke. You might think that the 108-yard field-goal return by the Bears was the low point for the 2006 Giants. Not even close. They managed to dive even deeper into the depths of raw badness two weeks later, on November 26, 2006, when they played the Tennessee Titans in Nashville.

The Giants played the first 50 minutes of the game like champions. The Titans looked like a defeated team. Tennessee came into the contest with a 3–7 record, and on this Sunday they looked lackluster, already defeated. The stands were quiet, as Titans fans seemed resigned to watching their team get thrashed again.

During the first three quarters, Big Blue's defense held the Titans scoreless, and the Giants had pushed into the end zone three times, once on a Manning pass to Plaxico Burress and twice with touchdown rushes by Brandon Jacobs.

Things started to go wrong early in the fourth quarter when, on second and four, Manning decided to throw long. The throw, intended for Burress, was off target and intercepted by Titans cornerback Adam "Pacman" Jones. Burress then made a seemingly

2006 GAME VS. BEARS

Giants Stadium, East Rutherford, New Jersey, November 12, 2006

	1	2	3	4	Total
Bears	3	7	14	14	38
Giants	7	6	7	0	20

Attendance: 78,641

half-hearted attempt to tackle Jones, who managed to return the ball all the way to the Giants' 46.

The drive appeared to be stopped when the Giants' defense forced a fourth-and-nine. The Titans went for it, with quarterback Vince Young scrambling to his right for seven yards, two shy of what he needed.

But Giants cornerback Frank Walker, who was playing because starter Corey Webster had an injured toe, hit Young after he went out of bounds. Young was hit in the vicinity of his head, and Webster was flagged for unnecessary roughness. The Titans had an automatic first down at the Giants' 6.

Three plays later Young threw to Bo Scaife for a four-yard touchdown pass. On the ensuing drive, the Giants failed to convert a third down and were forced to punt the ball. The Titans drove right back, with Vince Young running around right end for a one-yard touchdown to culminate a six-play drive.

The Giants were able to get one first down on their next drive but again had to punt. The Titans got the ball with a chance to tie and 2:58 left in the game. After three consecutive incomplete passes by Young, the Titans faced a fourth and 10 at their own 24 with no choice but to go for it.

That was when things got particularly painful for Giants fans. Young again dropped back to pass and appeared to be sacked by Giants rookie defensive end Mathias Kiwanuka. But the youngster, erroneously believing that Young had already thrown the ball, let go and allowed Young to run free. Kiwanuka had his head down and mistook a Young pump fake for a real pass. And by the time Young finished running, he'd gained 19 yards and a first down. Four plays later Young threw a 14-yard touchdown pass over the middle to Brandon Jones. There were 44 seconds left on the clock.

With the choke already in full gear, Manning made what may be remembered as the worst throw of his career. The Giants were on their own 28 with 32 seconds to go. Take a knee, and you go into overtime.

Instead, despite the fact that nothing had gone right for the past nine minutes of the fourth quarter, Coughlin decided his Giants should continue to be aggressive, to try to get in position to win it on a field goal in regulation.

Manning scrambled to his right and tried to throw to David Tyree on the right sideline. But the ball came out of his hand wrong. Instead of a tight spiral, the football moved with a sickening wobble. The pass came down well short of its target, and Titans cornerback Jones jumped to make the interception.

It was Jones's second interception of the quarter. The Titans took over on offense with one timeout left at the Giants' 49. With momentum so fully in their favor, there was no question that the Titans would go for a win right then and there. Young threw two quick complete passes to the sidelines, giving the Titans the ball at the Giants' 31. With six seconds left, the game was won by the Titans with a 49-yard field goal by Rob Bironas.

When it was over, the Giants were devastated.

"We are going to be sick about this one…forever," said Coach Coughlin. "It's a terrible shock for everyone in the organization. There's no excuse. There's no sympathy. There's no nothing. We're going to be sick about this one forever. It's a ridiculous thing to try and reassess."

Asked about Manning's final interception, the coach said, "There's no way you can throw an interception. There's no way. If you're rolling and you don't like what you see, throw it out of bounds. You can always go into overtime."

As the season had progressed Manning had shown a dangerous tendency to underthrow his receivers when he was forced out of the pocket. Twice during the fateful quarter that habit had hurt

2006 GAME VS. TITANS

LP Field, Nashville, Tennessee, November 26, 2006

	1	2	3	4	Total
Giants	7	14	0	0	21
Titans	0	0	0	24	24

Attendance: 69,143

the Giants badly, with Jones twice being the recipient of Manning's passes, which soared ungracefully through the air like recently shot pheasants. Manning, who was 16 for 21 for 130 yards through three quarters, went two for seven for just 13 yards and two costly interceptions in the fourth.

"It's a team we should've beaten the shit out of," said Jacobs. "The Titans stunk. We pissed it away."

"I could only imagine this happening in a nightmare... maybe," said center Shaun O'Hara. "What can you say? It's indescribable. I don't fault anybody for being at a loss for words. It's sick. It really is. It makes you feel sick."

Added linebacker Antonio Pierce, "I never thought they would go on to win the game until they won the game."

About his rookie mistake Kiwanuka explained, "The bottom line is I put a pass rush on, and I got to the quarterback. Unfortunately I made a bad decision. I thought he had thrown the ball. He started his passing motion. I put my head down to drive through him. I figured at that point it was going to be a 15-yard penalty for roughing the passer if I drove him to the ground. Obviously, I made a mistake, and it cost us the game." It was nice of the rookie to take the hit for the rest of the team, but everyone knew there was plenty of blame to go around.

The 2006 meltdown continued the following Sunday, when the Giants lost at home on a last-second field goal to the Dallas Cowboys. Although Manning played better against the Cowboys than he had in previous weeks, costly Giants errors continued.

Amid speculation that Coughlin's stint as Giants head coach was nearing an end, the team lacked discipline both on and off the field. Burress, criticized for being soft the previous week, was flagged for unnecessary roughness in this game. He also committed a purely mental error when he called for a timeout with a little more than a minute left to play in regulation at a time when it would have been to the Giants' advantage to let the clock run. That timeout allowed the Cowboys an opportunity to drive down the field and into field-goal range, where they had a shot at winning the game.

In a postgame press conference, Coughlin made it clear that the timeout had been called on the field and had not been called by him. Still, everyone knew where the buck stopped, and once again Coughlin had been embarrassed by his team's inability to maintain its composure. All in all, the Giants had been backed up 94 yards by penalties. Sixty of those yards came on personal fouls.

At that same press conference, Coughlin said, "We needed to win a football game. We had too many penalties. Dumb penalties. All four of these remaining games are very critical. We're going to stick together, and we are going to work as hard as we can. We're going to find a way to win. We lost a game which we had an opportunity to win, and nobody feels worse about it than I do."

Coughlin also received criticism for a fourth-quarter call when he decided to go for it on fourth down. The play sent running back Jacobs around the left end, but penetrating Dallas defenders dropped him for a loss and the ball changed possession. Many feel that, on short yardage situations like this one, when less than the length of a football was needed for a first down, a running back should always take a beeline for the line of scrimmage even if there are no visible holes to run through.

A season that only a month before had seemed to be destined for a division championship had now officially fallen apart. The Giants, with this loss, fell two games behind the Cowboys in the NFC East race.

As was true the week before, one of the most controversial plays in the game was made by Kiwanuka, who managed to turn a positive into a negative before Giants fans even had an opportunity to cheer. Kiwanuka intercepted a Tony Romo pass that had been deflected at the line of scrimmage, and then Kiwanuka ran down the field holding the ball out at his side like he didn't care for its smell. Predictably, the ball was slapped away from him before he was tackled, and although the Cowboys lost a little ground on the play, they were awarded a first down because they'd lost possession of the ball and then gotten it back. From that point the Cowboys drove down the field with the help of a 26-yard pass interference penalty to score their first touchdown of the game.

Perhaps it was no coincidence that the four-game slide by the Giants, which dropped their record from 6–2 to 6–6, coincided perfectly with the games Strahan missed because of his sprained foot.

The pattern of fourth-quarter collapses continued on December 17, when the Giants took on the Eagles in Giants Stadium. The Giants led the game 16–14 early in the fourth quarter, when Jay Feely kicked a 24-yard field goal.

On the next series, however, Brian Westbrook ran for a 28-yard touchdown right up the middle to give the Eagles back the lead. The Eagles were expected to pass, so the Giants' defense had

2006 GAME VS. DALLAS

Giants Stadium, East Rutherford, New Jersey, December 3, 2006

	1	2	3	4	Total
Cowboys	7	3	3	10	23
Giants	7	0	3	10	20
Attendance: 78,666					

2006 GAME VS. EAGLES

Giants Stadium, East Rutherford, New Jersey, December 17, 2006

	1	2	3	4	Total
Eagles	7	7	0	22	36
Giants	7	3	3	9	22

Attendance: 78,657

set up deep in the secondary. Instead the Eagles ran Westbrook right up the middle, and there were enough offensive linemen to block anyone who might have come close to tackling him. The Giants didn't give up then, though. They fought back once more.

Will Demps intercepted Jeff Garcia and ran the ball back to the Giants' 41-yard line before lateraling to R.W. McQuarters, who took the ball an additional 24 yards to the Eagles' 36.

Aided by a long pass-interference penalty, the subsequent drive came to a happy ending with Jacobs's one-yard touchdown plunge. The Giants again had the lead 22–21, with under seven minutes left on the clock.

Giants fans might as well have turned off their TVs right then and there. The rest was enough to pull their hearts out of their chests. The Giants' defense looked out of gas, and the Eagles marched through it, 80 yards in eight plays for a touchdown.

Now time was short and the Giants needed seven points to tie. But any chance went down the tubes when Manning threw an interception to Trent Cole, who returned the ball 19 yards for the final score of the game.

The Giants had allowed the Eagles to score 22 points in the fourth quarter, and Big Blue lost a game they had led with seven minutes left to go.

Because the 2006 NFC was so weak, the Giants, despite all their efforts, made the playoffs. Predictably enough, however, they were eliminated in the wild-card round. The true surprise was that Coughlin wasn't fired.

THE GREATEST RUNNER: TIKI BARBER

You might think of him as perfect. A gifted athlete. A lot smarter than your average football player. Better looking, too. A career in media ahead of him. The Frank Gifford of his day. But things haven't always been perfect for Tiki Barber.

The twin brother of Tampa Bay Buccaneers cornerback Ronde Barber, life wasn't all good when Barber was growing up. The biggest regret in his life, he says, is that he didn't grow up with a "consistent father figure."

In a 2006 interview, Barber said, "Obviously, my father was out of the picture. I had great father figures in my teachers and coaches, but they kept changing. But I don't regret any of it because it has given me a perspective on life and what kind of father I want to be. And it makes me appreciate how strong my mother is. She sacrificed 20 years of her life for us."

According to Barber, his father still emails every once in a while, but only to the address of Barber's wife because he knows his son won't respond.

Tiki and Ronde went to predominantly white schools growing up, and Barber says now that his biggest challenge as a youngster was to convince people that he had a brain. It was difficult to overcome the perception that he was "only" a great athlete. That task, he said, was made easier by the fact that he was a twin. His brother had essentially the same challenges. Tiki and Ronde approached life together as youngsters, and that made it easier.

Barber later recalled the moment in 1997 when he learned he'd been drafted by the Giants: "I was playing golf. My brother and I picked it up a couple of weeks prior. We didn't want to be sitting in front of the TV while our lives and futures were determined. We were playing Birdwood Golf Course in Charlottesville, Virginia. When we were done I got a phone call from Giants public-relations man Pat Hanlon. That was very weird because there was only one person in the NFL that I knew personally, and that was Pat Hanlon. When my wife's parents moved to Virginia from Vietnam, a preacher, Reverend Davenport, took them in, and that's Pat Hanlon's uncle. So Pat put Coach [Jim] Fassel on the

The greatest running back in team history: Tiki Barber.

phone. 'Hey Tiki, it's Coach Fassel. We're gonna take you with our next pick.' I was like, 'Who's Coach Fassel?'"

As a pro football player, Barber was a late bloomer. He'd been drafted in the second round of the 1997 NFL draft out of the University of Virginia. During the first three seasons, he was best known for his ability to fumble. He was also known as the "little" running back. At only 5'10" (maybe), he was hard for defenses to find.

In 1999 he played in all 16 games but gained only 258 yards on the ground. He first gained 1,000 yards in a season in 2000, and with the exception of 2001, when he only ran with the ball 166 times all year, he gained at least 1,000 yards every season for the remainder of his career.

In 2005 Barber gained an incredible 1,860 yards running the football. This is the Giants record by head and shoulders and one of the most productive rushing seasons in the history of the league. His highlight that year was a touchdown run from his own 5-yard line, a 95-yard touchdown gallop.

In addition to the more than 10,000 yards Barber gained running the ball during his 10-year NFL career, he also amassed almost 600 receptions for an additional 5,000-plus yards. And when he stopped fumbling, he stopped fumbling for good. His improved high-and-tight grip made it next to impossible for tacklers to punch the ball out.

In 2006 Giants fullback Jim Finn was asked what it's like to run interference for Barber. He replied, "It's a great honor being able to block for the greatest back in the storied franchise's history."

During the 2006 season, with the Giants facing the Buccaneers, Tiki and Ronde got to play against one another and even had contact, although no solid hits, on the field.

TIKI BARBER'S TWO GREATEST RUNS

In 2006 Tiki was asked what his greatest single run had been. Unable to narrow it down to one winner, Tiki proclaimed it a two-way tie. He said, "We played the Houston Texans. I think it was their expansion year [2002], and we ran a spring play to the right sideline, and I ran all the way over there. There was nowhere to go. This is back when I was young and spry, so I just reversed field all the way back, 53 yards to the other side of the field. Marcus Coleman was waiting for me on the sideline, and I had to navigate him somehow. So I stutter-stepped him a little bit, got him off balance, and then just threw him out of bounds, and then went 70 yards down the sideline. It took about 20 seconds, but I didn't score. My best scoring run was the 95-yarder I had against the Oakland Raiders, New Year's Eve, 2005. The Raiders knew what play we were running, and I could hear them saying to be ready for that play, which I took advantage of because I cut back against the grain, made the safety miss, then got escorted down the sideline by Plaxico Burress and Amani Toomer."

Before and during his 10th and final NFL season, Barber began to show an increased interest in working in media, everything from color commentary on TV football games to guest-hosting morning talk shows in New York City. During that 2006 season Barber announced that he would be retiring at the end of the year. He wanted to end his career while his body was still in good shape and his brain was still functioning crisply. He admitted that he had been heavily influenced by his family when making the decision to hang up his cleats.

The decision to announce his impending retirement during the season was a controversial one. He had, in essence, uttered the word *quit* while the battle was ongoing. The controversy only worsened when Barber (and the rest of the Giants, to be fair) went into a slump after the announcement.

Yet despite the fact that the Giants had been playing poorly, losing six of eight coming down the stretch, they still had a shot to make the playoffs. This was a testament to the overpowering mediocrity of the NFC in 2006.

The AFC had been whomping up on the NFC all year, to the point that an 8–8 record might earn the Giants a wild-card playoff berth if they could beat the Redskins in Washington in the final game of the season.

The Redskins, being an NFC team, could be beaten. But the Giants had not behaved like a team that wanted to win in several weeks. They had squandered leads, made dumb plays, and had generally proved spineless the instant they needed to demonstrate backbone.

Barber's retirement announcement and the slump had begun, more or less, at the same time. There were other reasons for the fade, too. Injuries were the largest factors. Coughlin's questionable leadership skills and Manning's shaky passing accuracy and decision-making were others. Barber's message that he was done with football and that he was looking forward to the glamorous— and soft!—world of show business hadn't done much for the adrenaline level of his teammates.

Two days before the season finale, Barber told the press, "My decision to retire is so far gone, it's not in my mind anymore." The

GIANTS' TOP SINGLE-GAME RUSHING PERFORMANCES

Of the seven occasions on which a Giants running back has gained more than 200 yards in a game, all but two were accomplished by Tiki Barber.

Date	Player	Yards	Score
December 30, 2006	Tiki Barber	234	Giants 34, Redskins 28
December 17, 2005	Tiki Barber	220	Giants 27, Chiefs 17
November 12, 1950	Gene Roberts	218	Giants 51, Cardinals 21
October 30, 2005	Tiki Barber	206	Giants 36, Redskins 0
December 31, 2005	Tiki Barber	203	Giants 30, Raiders 21
December 28, 2002	Tiki Barber	203	Giants 10, Eagles 7 (OT)
December 21, 1985	Joe Morris	202	Giants 28, Steelers 10

trouble was, Barber couldn't un-say something he had said. But he tried. "You guys know that this is not something that just happened, that sprung up when a reporter followed me around. I've been thinking about my after-football days for years." But because the public was aware that Barber's days on the gridiron were counting down, fans noticed when he began playing sluggishly, as if someone had dimmed his pilot light a notch or two. *New York Post* columnist Jay Greenberg said Barber had been a "walking, talking ghost" since the retirement announcement.

During the week before the Redskins game Barber was asked by a Washington reporter if the retirement buzz had hurt his game. He admitted to a certain loss of concentration, saying, "My focus has been fine during games. It drifts during the week, though. If I play like I've checked out, then I've checked out. I don't think I ever have." Answering unasked questions regarding his own tenacity during practice, the running back said, "You can call and ask Sean Payton. He used to get on me because he thought I was bored. It's just my approach, how I prepare. I'm lucky because I get things quickly." He then reminded the reporter that he was a very smart guy and that he would be available for job interviews from the media as soon as he was tackled for the final time.

Barber had not played well during his last game at Giants Stadium, a loss. If he was feeling nostalgic about his time in the Meadowlands, he did a great job of masking it for the public.

"It wasn't overly emotional," Barber said, referring to his last game in front of the hometown crowd. "I love this game, but it's a stepping stone in my life. The nature of the beast is I haven't known when my last game would be for 10 years. I could have walked down the stairs, broken my ankle, and never played again. Our jobs are unique, exciting, and fun in a lot of ways, but it's still a job. You enjoy it while you can."

So, going into the final game of the 2006 season against the Redskins, the Giants were in a must-win situation yet had little solid reason for hope. They had been playing poorly, and despite what Barber was saying, there was evidence that part of him had retired the moment his plans became public.

What Barber did was break his own Giants record for most yards gained in a game with 234, leading his team to a 34–28 victory over the Redskins and a berth in the playoffs. He accomplished the feat on only 23 carries, averaging greater than 10 yards per rush. He scored three times, from 55, 50, and 15 yards out. Some of it was great running, and some of it was lousy tackling. It was always Barber's style to exploit the other team's weaknesses, and in this case, the Redskins' weakness was their 30th-ranked defense.

"It's easy to say we don't have it," Barber said after the game, "but we believe we do."

"It's just what I expected from him in a game like that," said fullback Finn. "I figured in his last regular-season game he'd break some kind of record and carry us to a win. That's what he did."

"I just kind of shake my head," added guard Chris Snee. "I'm glad I was able to play with him, and I'm glad we have one more game together."

As it turned out, the Giants, who were mediocre and then some during the 2006 season, had made it into the playoffs because they played in a mediocre division in a mediocre conference. They had an 8–8 record. (I know, I know—you don't want to live in a world in which 8–8 teams make the playoffs, even if they are the Giants, but that's the way things are these days.)

The Giants lost to the Eagles in Philadelphia in the first round of the playoffs, the wild-card round, on a last-second field goal. But the brief playoff appearance gave Barber one more chance to play in a Giants uniform, even if it was the white with red numbers uniforms that rub old-time Giants fans so very, very wrong. (How can Big Blue wear red?)

As soon as Barber saw the ball sail through the goal posts to cinch the Giants' defeat and close the book on his football career, he headed out onto the field to shake hands with his Eagles opponents, in particular those he had faced for many years.

Then he retreated to the visiting locker room, where he spent an hour showering, dressing, and saying good-bye to teammates. Outside the locker room his friends and family were waiting for him. After he spoke to them he turned his attention to the press.

"I'm going to miss the things that I've become accustomed to in 10 years," Barber said. "Sitting in the meetings with my running-back guys, going out on the football field and having fun playing a kid's game and making a great living doing it. Yeah, I will miss that. But I think the sadness will be for quiet moments when I can sit and recollect."

Barber's last game was statistically spectacular. He rushed the ball 26 times for 137 yards and caught two passes for 15 more yards. But it was the type of performance Giants fans had grown used to, especially over the second half of Barber's 10-year career.

About Barber's retirement, Coach Coughlin, his own future uncertain, said, "It will be very sad to not see him put that Giants uniform on again."

Asked to comment on his coach, Barber returned the love, saying, "Coach Coughlin has done great things in his three years here. In particular last week, you see situations going askew. As a head coach, you have to make very difficult decisions. And he made a very difficult one by replacing [offensive coordinator] John Hufnagel two weekends ago. And that's what you have to judge him on."

Addressing his retirement, Barber said, "I don't have any regrets about retiring. It's a sport, it's a game. It's something I've loved and relished doing going back to when I was 10 years old. And now it's done."

Manning said, "Obviously we're losing our guy, our workhorse, the guy we give the ball to a lot. So obviously it's going to affect something, but we've just got to move on and other people have got to get better."

In 2007 Barber's future looked brighter than Big Blue's. On February 13, he announced that he had signed a contract with NBC to co-host their *Today Show* morning program and to appear on NBC's football telecasts in a to-be-determined capacity. NBC beat out ABC and Fox in the rush to sign him.

Even as he was announcing his latest career move he couldn't help but comment on the Giants, and again he spoke in that particular Barber way. He's a truth-blurter and is candid in a way most football players aren't. He came close to blaming Coughlin for prematurely ending his football career. "Couch Coughlin is very hard-nosed," Barber said. "And I didn't get a lot of time off. I couldn't sit down and rest myself. And so it was a constant grind—a physical grind on me that began to take its toll. The grind took its toll on me and really forced me to start thinking about what I wanted to do next. And that's not a bad thing. That's a good thing, for me at least. Maybe not for the Giants because they lose one of their great players, but for me it is. There would be days when I couldn't move on Tuesday or Wednesday at practice, and he'd get mad at me for going half speed. And I told him, 'Coach, I can't do it. I'm going to be out here. I'm not going to miss a practice, but I can't give you what you want all the time.' And he understood. We were in full pads for 17 weeks, and with the amount of injuries we had, it just takes a toll on you. You just physically don't want to be there when your body feels the way you do in full pads. And while the extra work probably doesn't have a really detrimental effect on how you practice or how you play, it has an effect on your mind. And if you lose your mind in this game, you lose a lot. And that's something Coach Coughlin needs to realize. He has changed in little ways, but I still think he needs to change more. The game has changed. Players are different. You have to understand them and get to know them in order to encourage and motivate them to be successful."

There's something slightly unsettling about Barber's opinion. It's hard to imagine football players of the past admitting that they retired because practice was too hard and the coach was to blame for the team losing one of its all-time greats—that is, the player himself. A stoic attitude is often required of a head coach. If Coughlin were racist or had another character flaw, the criticism would be justified. But the fact that he sees his players as employees and works them hard makes him, well, a football coach. It's just a little disappointing to listen to a football player who likes himself that much display such little regard for the organization that made him famous.

LEGAL WOES

Compared to some teams—(cough-Bengals-cough!)—the Giants' legal problems and off-field embarrassments have been few and far between. But they exist. Lawrence Taylor and Dave Meggett are two who made the papers in the ugliest of ways.

L.T.'S DESCENT INTO HELL

The most troubled ex-Giant has been the franchise's greatest player, the one and only Lawrence Taylor. His problem was drugs. Cocaine. Crack.

At the start of the 2004 NFL season Taylor was interviewed on CBS's *60 Minutes* to promote his book *LT: Over the Edge*. Regarding his cocaine addiction, which plagued him both during and after his football career, he said, "I'm recovering. Every day, I'm recovering. I think the likelihood of it happening lessens every day for me. Because, you know, my life is so much better." He admitted on the news magazine program that his addiction ruled him after he retired from football, that his daily expenditures on drugs and women added up to thousands of dollars.

As a player, L.T. admitted, he didn't always exhibit perfect sportsmanship. He saw football as a job, and the idea was to win. So he started looking for advantages even before the teams took the field. He said that he started working on his opponents days before the game was played, psyching them out and softening

HOW L.T. CAME TO BE A GIANT

The Giants drafted L.T. with the second-overall pick in the 1981 draft. The Saints had the first pick, and up 'til the last second, the Giants were convinced New Orleans was going to take L.T. They had been scouting him.

"I thought the Saints' defensive staff had convinced Bum Phillips to take Lawrence," remembered the late Giants general manager George Young. "But late the night before the draft, we learned the Saints were committed to taking George Rogers." And so Young picked L.T., who was issued No. 56.

them up. Along with playing with their heads by making comments to reporters, he would take a more active role in affecting their on-the-field performance. According to L.T., he used to hire call girls to visit his opponents on the night before a game to wear them out. And it *always* worked.

"You know what they like and what type of women they like, and you just call the service, 'What you got?' 'You keep the guy up just as long as you can,' were the girls' instructions. When a player says 'I got a game tomorrow. I got to get to sleep,' that's when the party really starts."

L.T. didn't make up the hooker trick. He only did it to others because it had been done to him before a big game against the Oilers.

"Knock on the door. You open the door, and you got two beautiful women. 'We're for you!' And I'm like, 'You're in the right place.' It worked on me. They did a pretty good job."

In the interview with *60 Minutes,* Taylor also admitted he once came to a team meeting in handcuffs. It wasn't that he was in trouble with the law, it was just that a couple of professional women he'd been with had been trying out some new equipment on him and had lost the key. A locksmith had to be called into the clubhouse so L.T. could practice.

Along with women, the biggest temptation for L.T. when he was a player was from the drug dealers. "They're handing out

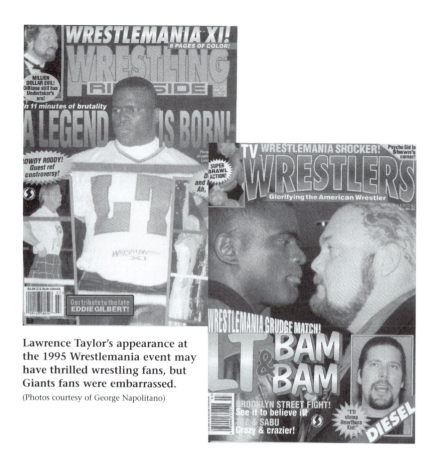

Lawrence Taylor's appearance at the 1995 Wrestlemania event may have thrilled wrestling fans, but Giants fans were embarrassed.
(Photos courtesy of George Napolitano)

free drugs because they want to get in," he said. "They want to be in your world. So everything is free while they're getting into your world. But once they get into your world, they take over your world. Now, it's their world. And you're just there, just a part of it."

L.T. said he first tried cocaine during his rookie season, 1981. By his third year in the league he had graduated to crack. "I'd go through an ounce a day. And at times I'd be standing in the huddle, and instead of thinking what defense we were playing, I'd be thinking about smoking crack after the game. Well, like well, you gotta understand though. It didn't affect my play," he said.

To pass drug tests he borrowed urine from teammates. The one time he flunked a team drug test it was because his teammate had also been using drugs. He failed a second drug test and was suspended for four games in 1988.

A third flunked test would have meant banishment from the league, and L.T. succeeded in staying off drugs for five years. As his playing days grew shorter he began to fantasize about retirement. No football meant no drug tests, which meant he could do all the cocaine he wanted. In his book Taylor admitted, "I saw coke as the only bright spot in my future. Because that's how powerful the drug is."

He smoked crack the day after his last game in 1994. He smoked crack the day the Giants retired No. 56. By 1996 his wife had divorced him and he was arrested in South Carolina for buying crack.

During early 1995, Giants fans were concerned when L.T. entered the world of professional wrestling. Some thought it a shame that he was degrading himself in the circus-like atmosphere of "sports entertainment." Some saw it as a sure sign that L.T. was desperate for money, that his lifestyle had caught up with him. In retrospect, at least some of the speculation turned out to be true. But there were other reasons for the move as well.

L.T. was addicted to the cheers, and he missed hearing them now that his playing days were behind him.

Pro athletes, stars usually, were common guest stars on pro-wrestling shows. A guy could earn a buck during the off-season,

BOUNTY HUNTERS

According to L.T., the Giants awarded "bounties" for causing injuries to opponents. Bonuses were paid to players for putting an opponent out of the game.

L.T. says, "That's just part of being the rough-and-tough football player. You get no pay for doing a cheap shot, but if I hit you straight up—we're going to get paid for that. That's part of life. It may be $500. It may be $1,000. That's big money back then."

and that had been true for years. Babe Ruth did a stint. Joe Louis, too. Even Muhammad Ali took an "airplane spin" from wrestler Gorilla Monsoon. So when news leaked that L.T. was going to join the grunt-'n'-grapple crowd for some schtick, Giants fans hoped it would be brief and ultimately not too sad. As it turned out, L.T. worked very hard and ended up putting on—by wrestling standards—a great show.

In February of 1995, WWF (now WWE) president Vince McMahon called a press conference at the Harley Davidson Café in New York City. The invitation stated that Taylor would be there and that there would be a major announcement. Pro wrestling press conferences don't usually draw that much attention outside the world of wrestling magazines and newsletters, but this one, with L.T. there, was different. Camera crews from the major networks jammed the room. McMahon got the press conference started with a long statement about how he planned to make pro wrestling even bigger and better in the future. McMahon then announced that the main event at the upcoming Wrestlemania XI would be the heavily tattooed Bam Bam Bigelow versus (drum roll, please) Lawrence Taylor.

L.T. took the microphone as cameras clicked. "First of all, I'd like to say that it is a pleasure for me to be associated with the World Wrestling Federation," Taylor said. "As far as Bam Bam goes, he's a big guy, a gifted athlete, but I made a lot of men who were bigger and better than him retire from football."

"My plan is to wrestle once and once only," L.T. said during the prematch hype. "Wrestling is a great sport. I'm used to doing dangerous things. I'm here to protect my honor. Regardless of what happens in Wrestlemania, overkill is unnecessary." L.T. insulted Bam Bam but refused to denigrate wrestling. "They're real athletes, and I don't mind working with real athletes," he said.

The New York Times reported Taylor was going to be paid $500,000 to wrestle. Taylor's agent was asked by a nosy reporter if L.T. wrestling should be interpreted to mean the ex-linebacker was broke. "As far as I know, Lawrence Taylor does not have any financial difficulties," the agent said.

L.T. FUN FACTS

Lawrence Julius Taylor was born on February 4, 1959, in Williamsburg, Virginia. He attended North Carolina and wore No. 98. Taylor set numerous defensive records there. His UNC jersey number was later retired.

In his NFL career he had more than 1,000 tackles, 132.5 sacks, nine interceptions, 134 interception-return yards, two touchdowns, 33 forced fumbles, 11 recovered fumbles, and 34 fumble-return yards.

L.T. was never afraid to play in pain. At one time or another in his career he played with torn shoulder ligaments, a detached pectoral muscle, a hairline-fractured tibia, and a broken bone in his foot.

Once a reporter asked L.T. what he could do that no other linebacker could do.

"Drink," he said.

Taylor reinforced the notion that money didn't have anything to do with his new career when he said he was wrestling because his kids thought it would be fun. He added that he didn't want to do anything that might jeopardize his ability to play golf and admitted that the wrestling gig was "all in fun."

So when Wrestlemania finally came and the arena filled, wrestling fans weren't expecting much. They'd been down this road before. The athlete would take one wrestling move, maybe a body slam, then cold-cock the bad guy with one punch—or worse, with one forearm smash.

So everyone was shocked when Bigelow and Taylor put on an impressive 15-minute show at Wrestlemania XI on April 2, 1995, at the Hartford Civic Center in Connecticut. L.T. entered the ring wearing a football jersey patterned to look, more or less, like a Giants jersey. Instead of a No. 56 on the chest and back, it read "L.T."

Both wrestlers entered with a sizable entourage. Bigelow came in with a herd of wrestling heels, and L.T. came with a crew of NFL players, including former teammate Carl Banks. From the opening bell, Bigelow and Taylor exchanged high-risk wrestling moves. There were pile-drivers and body slams and guys coming off the top ropes onto each other. Guys flew over the ropes and out of the ring.

The action itself spilled out of the ring and onto the arena floor. In the end, this being the main event at the biggest show of the year, it was Bigelow who went down and didn't get up—following a few flying elbows and a pair of devastating shoulder tackles—and it was L.T. who pinned his man for the victory.

Wrestling fans were pleased, but Giants fans were embarrassed. Even if Taylor had given the performance his best effort, it was still, well, just plain ugly.

According to L.T., after his Warholian 15-minute career as a wrestling legend, he stayed off drugs more than a year but resumed smoking crack in the fall of 1997.

Of the period following his 1997 relapse, Taylor said, "I had gotten really bad. I mean my place was almost like a crack house—not where you sold it, but I had a lot of stuff in my house. It was a hell of an expensive party, I tell you. You know what, it was a party that never ended. I started feeling doomed. You want out, but the disease won't let you out."

He was arrested twice in 1998, charged with buying crack in Florida and possessing drugs in New Jersey.

L.T. THE THESPIAN

After Wrestlemania Taylor decided to give acting a try. He played a football player with a volatile personal life in Oliver Stone's movie *Any Given Sunday*. He played himself in the Adam Sandler movie *The Waterboy*, and on the HBO series *The Sopranos*.

Also, that's L.T.'s voice you hear when playing *Grand Theft Auto: Vice City*. He's B.J. Smith, the former football player who says, "To succeed at the game of football, as in life, you've got to eliminate everything in your path in a blind rage."

"You gonna have to do something now because you could actually go do some time," Taylor remembered telling himself. "You know? And they made that clear. They was gonna lock me up. I finally got it. I actually wanted to work the program, make it work." He got out of rehab in 1999.

L.T. the wild man is gone. Now there lives Lawrence Taylor. "L.T. left a long time ago," Taylor said. "He's left the building. I took my earring off. I don't want my earring anymore because I'm tired of being L.T. I don't want to be L.T. no more. L.T. is good for the comic books. I like Lawrence Taylor. Lawrence Taylor can handle life a lot better than L.T. L.T. can play some helluva football, though. He's a helluva football player."

MEGGETT OUT OF CONTROL

Taylor doesn't have the monopoly on criminal records when it comes to ex-Giants. He's got some serious competition from Dave Meggett.

Meggett grew up in South Carolina and went to school both at Morgan State and Towson University. For the Giants he was a kick returner, a running back, a pass receiver, and one of Bill Parcells's favorite players.

Fans loved him, too, because he made plays. He was Mr. First Down. Plays that went to Meggett converted third-and-long situations and lengthened drives that might otherwise have stalled. He led the NFL in punt-return yardage with 582 yards in 1989 and 467 yards in 1990. That same year he was named to The Sporting News All-Pro team. In 1993 he accomplished a rare feat: gaining more than 300 yards rushing, receiving, and returning kicks.

His popularity was also because by NFL standards he was downright tiny. Meggett claimed to be 5'7", and he tipped the scales at 190 pounds. To the fans' delight, once or twice a season the Giants would run a halfback option play featuring Meggett, and he'd heave one down the field. He threw a total of five passes, and three of them resulted in touchdowns.

He had a 10-year NFL career, from 1989 to 1998, the first six of those years with the Giants. He was on the Giants team that

LEON "NOT SO" BRIGHT

Leon Bright was a Giant with a gimmick. He was the punt returner who never called for a fair catch—which is a lot like being someone who enjoys Russian roulette: there's no way the story can have a happy ending.

Between 1981 and 1983 Bright fielded 105 punts in a row without calling a fair catch. The 106th was a doozy. It came in November 1983, versus the Redskins. The Giants sent a 10-man rush at the Redskins punter, and by the time the high punt returned to earth and into Bright's hands, the Redskins' coverage team had him teed up and ready for destruction. The ball and two Redskins arrived at Bright simultaneously. Bright and the ball went in separate directions. Even Bright went in a couple of different directions before falling. The Redskins recovered, and Bright lay still as death on the turf. He had to be hospitalized with a severe concussion and an injured shoulder. He didn't play for the remainder of the season and never played for the Giants again. Bright did play two more years for the Buccaneers before calling it a pro career, but he had added the fair catch to his repertoire.

Happily, Bright was still active in football in 2007, as the new head coach of the Daytona Beach Thunder of the World Indoor Football League.

won Super Bowl XXV. When Parcells moved around, Meggett moved with him, which explains why his next stops in the league were with the Patriots and then the Jets.

By the end of his playing days, however, Meggett had also established himself as a guy who was battling off-field demons. During the 1990s, Meggett was charged twice with rape and once with soliciting prostitutes. The latter charge came during the winter of 1990, when he offered a female police officer $40 to have sex with him.

It appeared that Meggett had gotten his life together during the following decade. He was gainfully employed as the city recreation and parks director in Robersonville, North Carolina. But that all fell apart starting in 2004 when Meggett surrendered to authorities in Dedham, Massachusetts, where he was ordered jailed for failing to produce $191,600 he owed in child support. Then, during the summer of 2006, Meggett was arrested yet again and charged with second-degree rape. The charges were filed by Meggett's 27-year-old ex-girlfriend. She told police that they had broken up a year before and that he had broken into her home around midnight and had raped her.

In a statement to the press, Meggett thanked the town of Robersonville for the opportunity, adding that "it's apparent I will no longer be able to complete my duties with the town of Robersonville." At the time of the announcement Meggett was jailed at the Pitt County Detention Center on a $200,000 secured bond.

Other charges listed on Meggett's rap sheet include assault and theft.

CLASSICS FROM THE VAULT

In this last chapter you'll find a variety of classic Giants stories, including Kerry Collins's very, very bad Super Bowl, Joe Pisarcik's very, very bad fumble, and Alan Ameche's touchdown that birthed a national obsession.

SUPER BOWL XXXV: IS IT OVER YET?

It had been said before Super Bowl XXXV that the Giants were the worst team ever to make it to the Super Bowl. They'd caught opponents on bad days, taken advantage of breaks, and *somehow* had managed to make it as far as the NFL championship game.

But that was as far as it went. The smearing they took at the hands of the Ravens was so painful to watch that most Giants fans probably didn't stick around to the end of the game.

It might be news to you that the Giants picked up a first down on their last possession of the game, but it probably wouldn't shock you, either. That's kind of the way things were going. When fans finally turned off the TV and decided to go to bed, as early as the third quarter, perhaps, the outcome was assumed—there was no point in watching any longer.

The Giants were confident during the days leading up to the game. At least they seemed so. They'd heard about the Ravens' defense, and they'd seen what it could do to even halfway-decent offenses like their own. But they weren't buying into it.

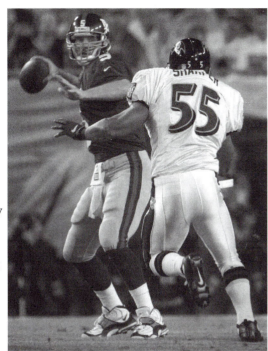

Giants quarterback Kerry Collins was the perceived goat of Super Bowl XXXV. After the game he said, "It's going to stay with me for a while. Obviously, I'm in a low state. This is the biggest game of my career and I didn't play well at all."

"We can definitely move the ball on this defense," Kerry Collins was telling his offensive linemen.

Confidence, even a little cockeyed confidence, had been a trademark of this team. The confidence—even the cockeyed part—came from the top, from head coach Jim Fassel. On November 22, with his team at seven wins and four losses and looking shaky following a miserable loss to the Lions, Fassel stood before the New York press and *guaranteed* that his team would make the playoffs. It made people think of Joe Namath's guarantee, and it seemed to a lot of people at the time that Fassel was setting his sights a little too high.

During the week before the Super Bowl, Fassel was asked about his bold prediction. Had he made it up on the spur of the moment? Did he plan to make the statement ahead of time? Did he anticipate the fuss that would ensue?

"When I called the staff together the night before to tell them what I was going to say, they thought somebody on the staff was going to be fired," Fassel recalled. "I just wanted to tell them what I was going to do, and the next day I did it. Just another part of my personality. I didn't do it for any other reason than it was in my gut. I needed to give my team some confidence, some fight, some direction, and get the focus on where we were going to go."

Fassel said that the current success dated back to the end of the 1999 season. The Giants had just finished 7–9, and Fassel wrote down a recipe, the things that needed to be done to turn the Giants into a winner. Fassel recalled, "It took me four, five, maybe six days to put together those 10, 15 pages the way I wanted them. We needed to go over every minute detail. We needed to change the players' approach to training camp. We needed to change the chemistry in that locker room—the guys we wanted to bring in and the guys we kept."

The team had not only kept Fassel's promise for him, but, behind Collins's solid arm, they'd marched all the way to the ultimate game. Why not feel confident?

Fassel's Super Bowl game plan was simple: a little bit of Tiki Barber's speed, sweeps, and dipsy-doodle, and then a lot of Collins's strong-arm throwing to fleet-of-foot wide receivers—Amani Toomer, Ike Hilliard—far downfield. That was the plan. It was apparent from the get-go that the game plan wasn't working, though, and confidence, cockeyed or otherwise, can be quick to crumble. Tiki's speed? In the first quarter Barber ran five times for five yards. The Ravens' secondary, singled out as suspect by the Giants, stuck to their receivers like glue. The Giants' receivers spent the whole game smelling the breath of the guys who were covering them.

Sometimes Collins threw the ball away on purpose because he was about to get creamed. Sometimes the passes were errant because he was forced to rush his throws. Sometimes the passes would hit the receivers right in the chest but the receivers would get flipped onto their heads and the ball would squirt out. And sometimes, many times, Collins's passes were tipped or batted down altogether by the uncaged lions of the Ravens' defense.

The frustration got to Collins quickly. On pass play after pass play the pocket would collapse around him, and he'd have to

SUPER BOWL XXXV STARTING LINEUPS

New York Giants Offense
Amani Toomer, WR
Lomas Brown, LT
Glenn Parker, LG
Dusty Zeigler, C
Ron Stone, RG
Luke Petitgout, RT
Ike Hilliard, WR
Ron Dixon, WR
Kerry Collins, QB
Greg Comella, FB
Tiki Barber, RB

New York Giants Defense
Michael Strahan, LE
Cornelius Griffin, LT
Keith Hamilton, RT
Cedric Jones, RE
Michael Barrow, MLB
Jessie Armstead, OLB
Emmanuel McDaniel, CB
Dave Thomas, LCB
Jason Sehorn, RCB
Sam Garnes, SS
Shaun Williams, FS

Baltimore Ravens Offense
Qadry Ismail, WR
Jonathan Ogden, LT
Edwin Mulitalo, LG
Jeff Mitchell, C
Mike Flynn, RG
Harry Swayne, RT
Shannon Sharpe, TE
Brandon Stokley, WR
Trent Dilfer, QB
Sam Gash, FB
Priest Holmes, RB

Baltimore Ravens Defense
Rob Burnett, LE
Sam Adams, LT
Tony Siragusa, RT
Michael McCrary, RE
Peter Boulware, LLB
Ray Lewis, MLB
Jamie Sharper, RLB
Duane Starks, LCB
Chris McAlister, RCB
Kim Herring, SS
Rod Woodson, FS

scamper right to avoid serious personal injury. Collins developed a terminal case of happy feet, and with good reason. Sometimes the Ravens caught him and threw him down, making Collins look like a rag doll as he slammed to the turf.

The Ravens' Ray Lewis hit people so hard they got up slowly, if they got up at all. And he hit somebody every play. He was in on just about every tackle, a madman. Giants fans remembered the days when they had a guy on defense whose fury dictated games, but the days of L.T. were long gone. Lewis was the man this day.

The Giants' offensive linemen were in for a shock. They'd planned on taking the defensive line out at the ankles, then begin looking for a linebacker to block. It didn't work out that way. Ravens defensive tackle Tony Siragusa didn't move no matter how he was blocked. And the other defensive linemen hopped, skipped, and jumped over the cut blocks.

At first the Ravens blitzed more often than was normal for them. Then they realized they didn't have to. The four-man defensive line was pressuring Collins just fine on its own.

One time Ravens defensive end Rob Burnett hit Collins so hard as he scrambled and rambled that the quarterback's helmet flew off, luckily without his head still inside it. Thinking he had been unnecessarily roughed, Collins got in Burnett's face. In a nanosecond he was surrounded by Ravens who looked like they might cook him and eat him.

About losing his composure, Collins later said, "It was stupid. That's not my game."

The Ravens scored first (and last, and most of the scores in the middle). The initial score of the game came eight minutes into the first quarter when, set up by a Jermaine Lewis punt return that took the Ravens into Giants territory, Trent Dilfer hit Brandon Stokley for a 38-yard touchdown pass. For his end-zone celebration, Stokley stood at attention and saluted.

The Giants appeared to have scored early in the second quarter when Jessie Armstead intercepted a Dilfer pass into the flat and returned it 43 yards for a touchdown. The play was nullified, however, by a holding penalty against defensive tackle Keith Hamilton. That was when things began to get extremely painful for Giants fans. Near excruciating. And, from that point on, the pain never let up.

With under two minutes left in the half, Dilfer's 36-yard pass to Qadry Ismail set up Matt Stover's 47-yard field goal.

The Giants got the ball back with time running out in the half and executed their most successful drive of the game. Highlighted by a 27-yard Barber run, the Giants pushed all the way to the Ravens' 29, their deepest penetration of the day. But that was as far as they got.

On the very next play Collins threw off his back foot toward Hilliard, who was double-covered in the end zone. The pass was intercepted by Chris McAlister, and the first half ended with the Ravens up 10–zip.

According to Barber, that was the single play that did the most to deflate the Giants' balloon. "We build our offense on big plays, and that was a big run that we had to get us into scoring position," Barber later said. "And then, the next play, all the wind is gone."

The pain continued in the third quarter when Collins threw an interception to Duane Starks, who returned the ball 49 yards for the touchdown. The pass had been intended for Toomer, but Starks stepped in front of the receiver for the pick.

By this time, according to *New York Times* columnist Dave Anderson, "In his desperation on the Giants' sideline, Jim Fassel resembled a magician who suddenly forgot how to do his tricks. When he reached into the top hat, there was no rabbit. When he waved his wand, nothing happened."

The lone highlight for the Giants came on the ensuing kickoff, which was returned 97 yards by rookie Ron Dixon for a touchdown. That got Giants fans' hearts pounding. It got hopeful fans thinking: "That's the shift in momentum we need to turn things around."

As it turned out, the Giants had the momentum for exactly one commercial break. The Ravens effectively negated the Giants' kickoff return by returning the next kickoff for a touchdown of their own—right back atcha!—with Jermaine Lewis running the ball.

Dixon was being treated for cramps on the Giants' sideline during the ensuing kickoff. He had to watch his own kickoff return nullified on the stadium's big-screen TV.

"I'm seeing this guy and he's still running," Dixon later said. "I'm saying, 'This can't be good.' After something like that, we have a return, and then they come back and return it. We didn't get anywhere with the return."

About his tit-for-tat touchdown Lewis said after the game, "When you take one kickoff back, the same guys that are on kickoff are on kickoff return. So I figured that they would be a little tired and that I could take advantage of it."

There were a little more than three minutes left in the third quarter, but the Giants clearly lacked the capacity to drive down the field, so outmatched were they by the Ravens' swarming defense, led by the game's MVP, Ray Lewis.

Lewis had an uncanny instinct for getting right into Collins's passing lane. When he wasn't threatening the quarterback's well-being, he was deflecting passes. After deflecting a total of 10 passes during the regular season, Lewis changed the direction of four of Collins's aerial attempts in the Super Bowl.

The Giants failed to move the ball in the fourth quarter, but the Ravens added two more scores. The Giants' defense, which had played tough early, now was tired and defeated. Jamal Lewis ran the ball in for a touchdown from three yards out six minutes into the fourth quarter, and after Dixon fumbled the kickoff and the Ravens recovered, Stover completed the scoring with a 34-yard field goal.

A look at the stats gives some idea of just how painful this game was to watch. There were 21 punts, 10 by the Ravens and 11 by the Giants. The Giants managed a total of 11 first downs during the entire game, and three of those came on penalties. For a team that scored 34 points, the Ravens' offense didn't perform for the most part either, earning only 13 first downs. The Giants had only 152 yards of total offense. The Ravens had 244.

After the game, still licking his wounds, Barber commented on how it had all gone so horribly wrong: "We felt coming in we had ways to attack them. Then once the game started, everything blew up. We made a ton of mistakes and missed assignments, things we hadn't done in the past seven weeks. It's because of the speed of their defense."

Giants offensive lineman Lomas Brown said, "They had a scheme to stop everything we had. I have never seen, in all of my years of football, such an athletic defense." Being a good team-mate, Brown added that it was unfair to scapegoat Kerry Collins for the defeat: "We didn't support him very well today. You can't blame it all on Kerry."

After the game Coach Fassel said, "We'll be back in this game. I'm disappointed, but I'm very proud of this football team. Nobody thought we'd be here. The way this team has handled the good and the bad, they'll handle this, too. That won't go away. This game will go away, but the way they handle things won't go away."

About his quarterback, he added, "I'm very proud of Kerry. He had a bad game, but he's a big-time quarterback and he can get us back in this game. We can get back here and win it."

Those were very kind words considering that Collins had just thrown four interceptions, including one that was returned 49 yards for a touchdown, and had completed just 15 of 39 passes for 112 yards. Phil Simms he wasn't.

"I felt that I wasn't prepared for the way they were disguising coverages," Collins said. "They really did a good job of that. Coverages were something that I didn't see very well. You can't see that on film."

The plan had been to pass to establish the run, he explained, saying, "We felt that we had to make them defend some of the passes to loosen them up. But we put our defense in a hole, and we have an outstanding defense.

"The Ravens' defense is as good as anybody I've ever played against. They play hard, they're quick, and they have a good scheme. You always imagine yourself on the plus-end of the turnover battle. We turned the ball over five times today. We gave them the ball five times, and they gave it back none. You just can't expect to win football games when you play like that."

Mike Freeman of *The New York Times* wrote, "What happened to the Giants in Super Bowl XXXV in trying to score on a brutal, intimidating Baltimore defense is what used to happen against opponents who boxed Mike Tyson. We are talking about the old-school Tyson, when his punch was the most feared in the sport and before he bit people's ears. Boxers used to enter the ring with plans against Tyson. Each thought he had found the antidote, the cure. But once that first punch landed square on his jaw, those

SUPER BOWL XXXV

Raymond James Stadium, Tampa, Florida, January 28, 2001

	1	2	3	4	Total
Ravens	7	3	14	10	34
Giants	0	0	7	0	7

Attendance: 71,921

plans would disappear in a painful haze, and someone like Frank Bruno would be staring at Tyson's black high-tops."

The two most loathed things in a football game, from a fan's point of view, are punts and incomplete passes. So even viewers without a strong rooting interest had plenty of reason to be unhappy. Bored to tears might be more like it.

Collins had a bad game, but Baltimore quarterback Trent Dilfer's day wasn't that much better; he completed only 12 of 25. The Ravens only gained 133 yards through the air for the game, which was only marginally better than the Giants' air attack, which netted only 86 yards.

Jamal Lewis was the only offensive player in the game whose stats were impressive. He ran the ball 27 times for 102 yards. Not spectacular, but 100 yards is usually considered a benchmark for ground success.

In contrast, Barber ran the ball 11 times for 49 yards. When the Giants fell behind, they abandoned their ground game, and that tendency allowed Collins to rack up the incomplete passes instead. Barber also was Collins's favorite receiver. Of Collins's 15 complete passes, six were to Barber for a grand total of 26 yards. Barber's longest reception was a whopping seven-yard gain. Clearly Collins didn't have anybody open downfield, ever, all day.

The four interceptions Collins threw tied a Super Bowl record. It's safe to say that, at least once before the big game, Collins imagined himself saying proudly that he was going to Disney

World. He imagined fans talking to him about his Super Bowl performance for years to come. But the Giants' performance had been so miserable and the game so difficult to watch that Collins now knew he didn't have to worry about fans talking to him about it. To mention it would be considered rude. The considerate fans were going to keep their mouths shut about Super Bowl XXXV and never mention it again.

Before the game Collins had been forced to address various personal and embarrassing issues. He'd had to explain that yes, he used to drink too much but now didn't drink at all. And yes, he once used a racial slur, but it was in jest. And yes, his desire to win was strong, and he never gave up as some people claimed. After the game, dealing with the press was no easier. Now he sounded like a man who had come to grips with the fact that, yeah, he was depressed, damn depressed.

"It's going to stay with me for a while," Collins said. "Obviously, I'm in a low state. This is the biggest game of my career, and I didn't play well at all. I'll go home. That's how I feel. I'll come back. I'll come back from this just like I've come back from other things."

What should get mentioned but doesn't is that the Giants overcame a lot of adversity in just getting to the Super Bowl, and for that job alone Coach Fassel deserved applause. And there was no real shame in being manhandled by the Ravens' defense. They had done the same thing to every team they'd faced all year long. They might have been the greatest defense in football history.

TAKE A KNEE, DAMMIT!

To understand the play, you've got to understand the dilemma the Eagles were in at Giants Stadium on November 19, 1978. Twenty seconds were left in the game. The Eagles were out of timeouts and behind 17–12. With no way to stop the clock, they probably had conceded victory to the Giants.

Giants quarterback Joe Pisarcik needed only to take a knee and the game was over. But somehow the Giants managed to snatch defeat out of the jaws of victory.

The call came in from Giants offensive coordinator Bob Gibson on the sideline.

"Pro 65 up."

What?

"Pro 65 up."

Gibson called a running play, a handoff to running back Larry Csonka (most famous as one half of the Miami Dolphins' "Butch Cassidy and the Sundance Kid" backfield with Jim Kiick.)

As the huddle broke up, Csonka's head reeled with the news that they were being asked to run an unnecessary play. He whispered in Pisarcik's ear, "Don't give me the ball."

Taking Csonka's advice was out of the question as far as Pisarcik was concerned. He had called a different play than the one sent in by Gibson once before that season, and Gibson had ripped Pisarcik a new one after the game. Pisarcik was not going to make that mistake again. Pro 65 up Gibson wanted, so pro 65 up he was going to get.

What could go wrong? Well, here's what.

Giants center Jim Clack snapped the ball to Pisarcik, who never completely controlled it. The ball bounced off of Pisarcik's suddenly metallic hands. He bobbled it for a moment.

Let's pause the tape right there and remember that Pisarcik has mishandled the snap. All he needs to do is fall on the ball and the clock will run out. Even if the referees call the play a sack and stop the clock, time will wind down once officials have respotted the ball. The Eagles are out of timeouts, and time will expire before a delay-of-game penalty would be called—and even if a delay-of-game penalty were called, so what? Okay, restart the tape.

The ball was still between Pisarcik's hands, sort of, and he might have controlled it eventually if not for two things. First, he attempted to gain control while whirling to his right so he'd be in the correct position to make the handoff. Second was the shock-and-awe force of Csonka, whose movement was in the correct rhythm to the play, while Pisarcik was out of synch. Csonka got to Pisarcik while Pisarcik was still bobbling the ball, and Csonka brushed the ball ever so slightly with his shoulder as he flew past. The quarterback brought the ball down and tried to hand it off to

Eagles safety Herman Edwards (46) grabs a fumble by Giants quarterback Joe Pisarcik and returns it for the game-winning score on the final play of the infamous November 19, 1978, contest.

Csonka's hip, and that finally transformed Pisarcik's bobble into a full-fledged fumble. The ball fell to the ground and bounced once off the hard Giants Stadium turf.

The Eagles' Herman Edwards snatched the bouncing ball out of the air and ran untouched into the Giants' end zone. The game was over, and somehow, some way, the Giants had lost.

As Edwards later remembered it, the Eagles had hardly even huddled before the play. They were getting ready to shake hands and hit the showers. Get 'em next time.

Clack, the Giants' center, recalled another aspect of the play that no one else remembered. Because of the confusion getting the unexpected play in from the sideline, the Giants had taken way too much time in the huddle. As the offensive line finally got set at the line of scrimmage, Clack looked up at the play clock and saw that it was running down. Forgetting that a fumble was a hell of a lot worse than a delay-of-game penalty, Clack claims he snapped the ball early, which was at least part of the reason Pisarcik had trouble handling it.

For Edwards it was a great moment because he had been the player burned on one of Pisarcik's two earlier touchdown passes. In later years, when he was head coach of the New York Jets, who also play at the Meadowlands, Edwards would always walk out onto the field before the game and put his foot on that spot where he recovered the fumble and won the game in the last seconds. It was his way of reminding himself that anything could happen and the game was never over until the last second had ticked off the clock.

After the game, the Eagles' happy, happy coach Dick Vermeil had to admit that he never saw the play. Convinced that the loss had become a matter of inevitability, he had stopped watching and was readying himself to march across the field and shake John McVay's hand.

Vermeil saw his team cheering and celebrating but saw none of the play. He had to be told about the fumble and Edwards's touchdown before he, too, could join in the celebration. The Eagles were the only ones in the stadium making any sound whatsoever. Giants fans were silent.

Pisarcik was deservedly the game's goat. Although the decision to call a play when no play was necessary was not his, he was the one who had failed to handle the snap and then turned a small error into a whopper.

The goat was a man people liked. There were no just desserts involved. He'd come from a coal-mining family in Wilkes-Barre, Pennsylvania. He was a star quarterback at New Mexico State and was known as a happy-go-lucky fellow.

The Giants had picked up Pisarcik as a free agent after he served a stint with Calgary in the Canadian Football League. He was signed by the Giants in March 1977, and reported to Giants camp that year as the fifth quarterback on the depth chart. The Giants had 13 wide receivers in camp, and they needed a lot of arms out there in practice to keep everyone busy. Pisarcik was not expected to make the team, but had an impressive preseason and survived every cut.

Immediately following the horrifying loss to the Eagles, Pisarcik realized his blunder had been so huge and had taken place in such a bright spotlight that it threatened to become career-defining. He hid in the trainer's room after the game, not wanting to face the press. Former Giants star and then director of operations Andy Robustelli convinced him to come out and make a statement.

"Joe, what happened out there?"

"I never had control of the snap," he said. He looked about to weep.

If Pisarcik was worried about career-defining, Coach McVay was thinking about career-ending. Calling a running play instead of a knee was the sort of thing that could get a coach fired. Right then and there. On the spot.

McVay faced the press like a man.

"Coach, what happened out there?"

"That's the most horrifying ending to a ballgame I've ever seen," McVay said.

Everyone sensed it. The ending to the 1978 Eagles–Giants game had been *horrifying*—horror of legendary proportions. It was history. Kind of a burning, ulcer-inducing history, but history nonetheless.

McVay kept his job for the time being, despite saying that responsibility for the blunder was, because he was the head coach, 100 percent his. It was at him that the buck stopped.

McVay had become the head coach of a New York pro sports team only after a long climb through the coaching ranks. He had coached at several high schools in Ohio, at colleges (as assistant coach at Michigan State, then head coach at the University of Dayton), and in the pros as head coach the Memphis Southmen of the World Football League before joining the Giants in 1976. In college at Miami University, McVay had been a star offensive lineman.

Despite taking the blame in public like a mensch, McVay hadn't actually made the mistake. And so, within days of the game, offensive coordinator Gibson—the man who called "pro 65 up" instead of "drop to ground in a fetal position and thank God for this glorious victory"—was given his pink slip.

Robustelli said that it would be a lie to say Gibson was fired just because of the fumble, although it helped. The Giants' director of operations said the firing stemmed from a "culmination of things." Then Robustelli announced that he himself would be retiring on December 31, 1978. (Although, to be honest, Robustelli had been considering retirement from football for a while anyway because outside business interests were taking up more and more of his time.)

Gibson was eventually asked the key question: *why*?

And he had an answer. He pointed out that the part of the story that everyone leaves out is that Pisarcik did take a knee on the play before the fumble. But the unnecessary roughness rules were different back then, and players were not as well protected and a let-the-boys-play feeling existed. On that previous play the Eagles' middle linebacker had blasted into Clack and sent him flying. That resulted in some pushing and shoving after the whistle down there in the trenches.

Gibson said he was reluctant to ask Pisarcik to take a knee a second time because he felt the two teams were on the verge of having a brawl. Therefore, he called a real play. If the Eagles didn't want to lose the easy way, they would lose the hard way. They'd be forced to make at least one more tackle. Obviously the potential disaster of a play gone desperately wrong never occurred to Gibson.

That was about it for the Giants that year. Losing a game like that is not the sort of thing you recover from. They had started the season 5–3, had dropped to 5–6 by the time they played the Eagles at Giants Stadium, and won only one more game (over the helpless St. Louis Cardinals), finishing 6–10.

Eight days after the final game, McVay was fired, joining his former offensive coordinator in the unemployment line. McVay had been the Giants' head coach since halfway through the 1976 season. His record at the helm was a dismal 14–23. After the Giants, McVay went to work in the 49ers' front office.

15 YEARS OF LOUSY FOOTBALL, WE'VE HAD ENOUGH

When the Giants are playing good football and trying hard, Giants fans are the most supportive in the NFL. But when there are prolonged periods of stinking the place up with prospects for the future looking dismal, Giants fans have been known to react appropriately. When things are revolting, they revolt.

Such was the case for the final home game of the 1978 season. Many people protested by staying home. There were more than 24,000 empty seats—although, as usual, every ticket was sold.

During the game a small plane cruised in a circle overhead, towing a sign that read, 15 Years of Lousy Football, We've Had Enough. Additionally, someone brought a dummy labeled "Wellington Mara," and it was hung in effigy.

Fans looked at the sign and did the math in their heads. Yup, last post-season appearance was 1963. If you wanted to count only NFL championships, the drought was longer than that. The Giants hadn't won it all since the second Sneakers Game in 1956.

After the game a reporter asked Mara if he had seen the plane.

"No," Mara said.

"Did you hear about it?"

"Yes, I heard about it."

"What do you think?"

"I didn't think," Mara snipped.

As we now know, the plane flying over the stadium did not shame the Giants into becoming a winner. The same kind of performance fans had grown used to continued until the Bill Parcells era. Here's a stat: the Giants were a combined 29–72–1 between 1973 and 1979.

To this day Edwards hears about that play from fans. It was a defining moment in his playing career as well.

"There are two versions of the story," Edwards says. "One is, 'I was at the game.' And that can't all be true because there weren't enough people at the game for all the times I've heard it. The second is they know where they were. They'll tell you, 'I was in a mall standing in front of the TV,' or, 'I was in the parking lot. I turned the radio on and heard what happened.' We won the game at the end, and we went on to the playoffs. The next thing, we're playing in the Super Bowl [two years later]. You see that in sports. One play gets you feeling like you have confidence. You're not worried about losing anymore; now you're thinking about how you can win."

Following the 1978 season, Tim Mara spoke up. He and his uncle Wellington had been disagreeing on who should be hired to fill the team's vacancies. To a reporter, Tim said, "I want us to have a winner. Wellington wants us to have a winner, his way. But Wellington's way has had us in the cellar for 15 years." The man eventually hired to replace McVay was 37-year-old Ray Perkins, a former wide receiver for the Baltimore Colts.

The beginning of the new age for the Giants began during the spring of 1979, when, in the first round of the draft, the Giants chose—drum roll, please—from Morehead State, Phil Simms. You should have heard the boos. Morehead State? Where's that? Kentucky? Never heard of it. Who did Giants fans want them to pick? Why, Jack the "Throwin' Samoan" Thompson, the quarterback out of Washington State, of course. Now there was a guy with an arm. (Thompson, by the way, went to the Bengals. He played in 51 NFL games over six years, four with Cincinnati and two with the Buccaneers. His career quarterback rating was 63.4.)

Flash ahead now to the end of the 1980 season, a little more than two years after the worst ending to a football game in New York Giants history. The Philadelphia Eagles, the benefactors of Pisarcik's blunder, took Pisarcik himself off the Giants' hands in exchange for a middle-round draft choice.

Pisarcik's new job would be as backup to the Eagles' starting quarterback Ron "Jaws" Jaworski. Pisarcik said he was "very happy" about the trade. Standing on the sideline in Philadelphia, after all, was a lot more fun than lying flat on his back on the turf of Giants Stadium.

At the ripe old age of 27, Pisarcik's days as a starter in New York seemed to be over anyway since the Giants had drafted

GIANTS WON-LOSS RECORDS, 1964-83

Year	Record	Year	Record
1964	2–10–2	1975	5–9–0
1965	7–7–0	1976	3–11–0
1966	1–12–1	1977	5–9–0
1967	7–7–0	1978	6–10–0
1968	7–7–0	1979	6–10–0
1969	6–8–0	1980	4–12–0
1970	9–5–0	1981	9–7–0
1971	4–10–0	1982	4–5–0
1972	8–6–0		(strike-shortened season)
1973	2–11–1	1983	3–12–1
1974	2–12–0		

Simms. After learning about the trade, Pisarcik said, "I could always look over my shoulder and see Phil Simms. I was made to feel I was just there from the old regime. Now they're really making a clean sweep."

Pisarcik had played a whole season with a porous Giants' offensive line, which surrendered 14 sacks in the first two games of the season. Now he felt "used" by the new Giants coach taking the hits while the team retooled for the Simms era.

Pisarcik only played four games for the Giants in 1979 before Perkins felt Simms was ready to make his debut, but in that short time Pisarcik had taken so many hits that he had a bruised shoulder, bruised ribs, and bruised knees. He was one gigantic bruise.

Sore or not, Pisarcik was upset at being replaced by Simms. "I don't think I should lose my job to a kid who hasn't learned to shave yet," he said. "In this business, you always have to step on somebody's toes. It happened to me. What can you do? Bottom line is I don't think Phil Simms is as good as me. I don't think he can throw as good as me."

Willing to disregard Simms, Pisarcik was considerably more polite when discussing Perkins, saying, "Perkins is a great coach

WHAT'S IN A NAME?

As is the case with some Civil War battles, the name of the Pisarcik incident varies depending on which side you are on. Giants fans tend to call it the Fumble, with a capital F. Eagles fans call it the Miracle at the Meadowlands.

and a great man, and I have no doubt he is doing what he thinks is best for the team."

He was also kinder to Jaworski, who would be starting in front of him in 1981. Pisarcik said, "I tried to call Jaworski yesterday to tell him that no matter what I did in summer camp or in the pre-season that I thought he deserved to be the number-one quarterback and that I hoped to help him all I could and make him the best quarterback he could be. I've never said this before in my life, but I think Ron is a good quarterback, and he has grown with the team and the team has grown with him. I'm not saying he's better than me—no player should ever say that—but he deserves to be number one."

About the trade, Perkins said, "I think it will work out well for both sides. I think Joe will be an excellent backup for them, and I wish them well. We got something that can help us in the future."

Pisarcik noted that his most famous play did allow the Eagles to win a game once, a game that helped Philadelphia make the playoffs in 1978, but he also noted that some of his best games ever were against the Eagles. In the opening game of the 1979 season he completed 20 of 40 passes for 274 yards. Even in the "Fumble game" he threw two touchdown passes. Pisarcik's first NFL start was in 1977 versus the Eagles, and he threw an 80-yard touchdown pass to Jimmy Robinson.

With Pisarcik gone, the Giants were still bad. When head coach Bill Parcells came on board in 1983 and led the team to a 3–12–1 record, the Giants had been through 20 years of retooling, so there was not much reason to think that this latest retooling would be any different.

THE GREATEST GAME EVER PLAYED—UNLESS YOU'RE A GIANTS FAN

The 1958 NFL championship game is recalled by those who were there—and by the many millions more who were watching on black-and-white TVs—as the Greatest Game Ever Played. It is the game that is credited with causing the explosion in pro football's popularity that led to today's Super Bowl culture. Before this game, pro football was a Sunday version of the Saturday college game. After this game, the NFL was a national obsession.

Until 1956 all football telecasts were local. But in 1956, selected games were shown on network TV for the first time, though games were never televised in their home city because it was thought to discourage ticket sales. That rule stayed in effect until 1973, when it was declared illegal by Congress. It was no coincidence that the Redskins were good at the time the rule changed, because it was Congress's own inability to watch games

Colts running back Alan Ameche scores the winning touchdown in overtime of the 1958 NFL championship game.

played in Washington that brought about the change. After that, games were only blacked out in the home city if the game was not sold out. Consequently, while fans around the nation watched this "greatest game," fans in New York listened to it on the radio and later watched the filmed highlights repeatedly. For live TV you had to go to a motel with an antenna on the roof, one that could get the TV signal from Connecticut.

The championship game was the second time the Giants and Colts had met that year. The Giants beat the Colts earlier, handing Baltimore one of only three defeats that season. Despite that, the Giants knew better than to take the Colts lightly. Baltimore had the best offense in the league and averaged more than 30 points per game.

The game was played at Yankee Stadium in front of 64,185 fans—and the crowd got quiet early. After Pat Summerall gave the Giants a 3–0 lead with a 36-yard field goal, twice in the first half Giants hero Frank Gifford coughed up the football, and both turnovers resulted in Colts touchdowns. The first came on a two-yard run by Colts running back Alan Ameche. The second came on a 15-yard touchdown pass from the great Johnny Unitas to Raymond Berry. The Colts led 14–3 at the half.

The turning point came in the third quarter, when the Colts drove the ball down the field all the way to the Giants' 1, but could not punch it in. Three times they held the Colts, and, on fourth down, the handoff to Ameche was rudely interrupted by a charging Chip Livingston, who arrived at Ameche not long after the handoff did, and the Giants took over at their own 5.

From there Charley Conerly led the team 95 yards for the touchdown.

The big play on that 95-yard drive was a 62-yard completion from Conerly to Giants speedster Kyle Rote. Rote was hit hard and fumbled at the Colts' 25, but running back Alex Webster, following up the play, picked up the loose ball and ran it to the Colts' 1. From there, Mel Triplett ran the ball in.

The Giants quickly regained the ball and again drove down the field. Conerly connected twice in a row with Bob Schnelker for 17 and 46 yards. The Giants then scored on a 15-yard pass

THE CRAZY FAN

Frank Gifford injured his knee in a game earlier in the 1958 season, and the injury was sufficiently severe to warrant an overnight stay in the hospital.

While in his hospital bed, with his leg immobilized, a stranger entered his room and said, "What's the matter with your Giants? What's the matter with all of you, Gifford? What you need is someone like me. A killer. I was in Korea."

Gifford surreptitiously armed himself with a water pitcher and said, "If you really think you can help the team, get down to Yankee Stadium and show them what you can do."

That seemed like a good idea to the guy, and he left. The man took Gifford's advice and went to the Giants locker room just as the team was suiting up for practice. He began screaming at the players and had to be removed by security.

His parting words were, "All right, so you don't appreciate me. I'll go down to Baltimore to help Johnny Unitas out."

from Conerly to Gifford. That gave the Giants a 17–14 lead early in the fourth quarter.

The Colts started their final drive at their own 14 with less than two minutes remaining. If there were still football fans who weren't familiar with the two-minute drill, Unitas gave them a lesson right then and there. He drove the team down the field efficiently, throwing crisp, short passes that were getting out of bounds and moving the chains. The Colts' Steve Myhra kicked the 20-yard game-tying field goal with seven seconds left on the clock.

To give you an idea of how new the concept of overtime was in pro football, when the fourth quarter ended and the game continued, many of the players were stunned and couldn't figure out what was going on.

Sam Huff recalled, "Nobody had ever talked about sudden death in a football game. We finished the game 17–17, and we're standing on the sideline trying to figure out how much money we get. Because you tied you figure you get half the money, which in

1958 NFL CHAMPIONSHIP GAME

December 28, 1958, Yankee Stadium, New York

	1	2	3	4	Overtime	Total
Colts	0	14	0	3	6	23
Giants	3	0	7	7	0	17

Attendance: 64,185

The winning touchdown became one of the most famous film clips in NFL history. Ameche ran helmet-first through a hole the size of Rhode Island a little more than eight minutes into the first overtime period in NFL championship game history, and the Colts were champions. Final score: Colts 23, Giants 17.

those days wasn't very much money anyway. So over comes the referee, and he says, 'Okay, here's the deal.' We're kind of all around him. 'What do you mean, deal?' 'Here's the deal: in three minutes, we're going to flip the coin again, and the first team that scores wins the game.' Sudden death. It was the first time I'd heard the words sudden death on a football field. I said, 'I'm tired, man. I just finished playing a football game.'"

It wasn't just the first overtime in a championship game, it was the first overtime in any NFL game that counted. They had experimented with overtime for preseason games in 1955, but that was about it.

The Giants won the coin flip, the offense went three and out, and Baltimore took over the ball at their own 20. The Giants' defense had not looked good against the Colts' offense late in the fourth quarter, and the task of stopping Unitas must have seemed daunting to a bunch of guys who were, let's face it, gassed.

The Colts went 80 yards in 13 plays. Unitas began with a handoff to L.G. Dupree that gained 11 yards. An eight-yard pass to Ameche and a 21-yard pass to Berry earned the Colts first downs. The ball was now on the Giants' 43.

On the next play the Giants' defense looked exhausted. The offensive line exploded off the ball and blew back the New York defenders. Ballcarrier Ameche was 20 yards downfield before the Giants' secondary could take him down.

A quick pass to Berry put the ball on the Giants' 8. Another short pass from Unitas to Colts tight end Jim Mutscheller put the ball on the 1-yard line. The Giants' defense recalled their goal-line stand of earlier in the game, the one in which Livingston made the spectacular play on fourth down—and they tried to summon up the strength from that success to do it again.

But no.

BIBLIOGRAPHY

Allen, Maury. "Toots Shor: The Movie," TheColumnists.com, May 10, 2006 (accessed October 31, 2006).

Anderson, Dave. "Giants Not a Dynasty, Just Champs," Nytimes.com, January 29, 1991 (accessed January 6, 2007).

———. "Mara: A Grand Old Name Again," Nytimes.com, January 27, 1987 (accessed January 6, 2007).

Associated Press, "Jim Fassel Wasn't a Happy Man Monday," January 7, 2003.

Branch, John. "Giants, Playing Catch and Release, Fail Again," Nytimes.com, November 26, 2006 (accessed November 7, 2006).

CBSNews.com, "Former Football Great Lawrence Taylor Tells Mike Wallace about Tricks He Used to Beat His Opponents on and off the Field," September 12, 2004 (accessed November 1, 2006).

Ditka, Mike, and Rick Telander. *In Life, First You Kick Ass.* Champaign, Illinois: Sports Publishing L.L.C., 2005.

Effrat, Louis. "58,836 Fans See Chicago Bow, 47–7," *The New York Times*, December 31, 1956.

Eisen, Michael. "Giants over Eagles in OT, 30–24," Giants.com, September 17, 2006 (accessed February 1, 2007).

———. *Stadium Stories: New York Giants.* Guilford, Connecticut: The Globe Pequot Press, 2005.

Fleisher, Walter. "Basketball Shoes Prove Big Aid to the Giants on Frozen Gridiron." *The New York Times*, December 10, 1934.

Freeman, Mike. "Ravens' Might Makes Right," Nytimes.com, January 29, 2001 (accessed January 6, 2007).

George, Thomas. "By Altering Attitudes, These Giants Have Become a Team," Nytimes.com, January 28, 1987 (accessed January 6, 2007).

Gola, Hank. "A Super Time: Two Decades Later, Big Blue Feels Spirit of '86," *The Daily News*, January 28, 2007, 80–81.

Greenberg, Jay. "Blueprint for 'D'-feat," *New York Post,* December 18, 2006, 80.

———. "The Final Daze: It Looks as if Barber Has Already Started Retirement," *New York Post*, December 29, 2006, 115.

Katz, Michael. "Eagles Get Pisarcik for a Draft Choice," *The New York Times*, April 24, 1980, D19.

———. "Twenty Seconds Left as Eagles Win," *The New York Times*, November 20, 1978, C1.

Koppett, Leonard. "Giants Top Redskins, 35–33, on 21-Point 4th Period," *The New York Times*, November 16, 1970, 64.

Litsky, Frank. "Giants Rout Broncos in the Super Bowl." Nytimes.com, January 26, 1987 (accessed January 6, 2007).

Loverro, Thom. *Eagles Essential: Everything You Need to Know to Be a Real Fan*! Chicago, Illinois: Triumph Books, 2006.

———. *Hail Victory: An Oral History of the Washington Redskins*. Hoboken, New Jersey: John Wiley & Sons, Inc., 2006.

Maaddi, Rob. "NY Giants 30, Philadelphia 24, OT," Associated Press dispatch, September 17, 2006.

Moran, Malcolm. "'Maybes' and 'Buts' Aren't Bothering the MVP," Nytimes.com, January 29, 1991 (accessed January 6, 2007).

Myers, Gary. "After the Catch, the Fall," *Daily News*, January 28, 2007, 82–83.

———. "Clock Ticks on Coughlin," *Daily News*, December 4, 2006, 54.

———. "Road Goes through Chicago," *Daily News*, November 13, 2006, 58.

New York Times News Service, "Joe Theismann Faces the Hit That Ended His Career," December 27, 2005, 20.

O'Donnell, Chuck. "Chuck Bednarik: The Game I'll Never Forget," *Football Digest*, March 2001.

———. "Jim Taylor: The Game I'll Never Forget." *Football Digest*, September 2002.

Picker. David. "Barber Leaves His Mark on Giants and Moves on to a New Career," Nytimes.com, January 8, 2007.

Reichart, Pat. "Quittin' Tom," *New York Post*, February 14, 2007, 88.

Schwartz, Paul. "Giants Stunned by Sickening Collapse," *New York Post*, November 27, 2006, 92.

———. "Whew! What a Relief! Tiki's Three TDs All but Assure Playoff Berth," Newyorkpost.com, December 31, 2006.

Shapiro, Leonard. "The Hit That Changed a Career: 20 Years Later, Theismann Reflects on Incident," *Washington Post*, November 18, 2005, E1.

Sheehy, Kate, and Bill Hoffmann. "Giant's Revenge on Brawl St.: Mara's Son Tackles Mocking Eagle Fan," *New York Post*, December 20, 2006.

Staple, Arthur. "Giants Collapse in Loss to Titans," Newsday.com, November 27, 2006 (accessed November 27, 2006).

Starr, Michael. "'Must See' Tiki: Scores NBC gig," *New York Post*, February 13, 2007, 3.

Thomas, Robert McG., Jr. "Giants Win Super Bowl with Nail-Biting Finish," Nytimes.com, January 28, 1991 (accessed January 6, 2007).

TV Wrestlers, "Wrestlemania XI Press Conference," July 1995, 60–62.

Vaccaro, Mike. "Unhappy Returns: Questionable Field Goal Doomed Jints," *New York Post*, November 13, 2006, 94.

Vacchiano, Ralph. "Tiki Torches Washington: Sets Giant Record to All But Lock Up Spot," *Daily News*, December 31, 2006, 113.

Wrestling Ringside, "Wrestlemania XI Rocks Nation," July 1995, 37–44.

Young, Bryant, with Allen St. John. "Snap, Crackle, Aauuggghhh!" *Maxim*, February 2000.

ABOUT THE AUTHOR

Michael Benson, a Giants fan for 45 years, is old enough to remember Tittle but not Conerly. He has previously written or cowritten 43 books, including *Joe DeLamielleure's Tales from the Buffalo Bills*, *Everything You Wanted to Know About the New York Knicks*, *Dream Teams*, *Ballparks of North America*, and *Hank Aaron: Baseball Player*. He has also written biographies of Wayne Gretzky, Jeff Gordon, Dale Earnhardt, and Althea Gibson. He is the former editor of *All-Time Baseball Greats*, *Stock Car Spectacular*, and *Fight Game* magazines. Originally from Rochester, New York, Benson graduated from Hofstra University with a B.A. in communication arts. Today he lives with his wife and two children in Brooklyn, New York.